Fundamental English Grammar with Short Readings

Keiichiro Fukui
Margaret Yamanaka
Nagaki Kitayama

Asahi press

Fundamental English Gramma with Short Readings
Copyright © 2019 by Asahi Press

All rights reserved. No part of this book may be reproduced or transmitted in any form or by any means, electronic or mechanical, including photocopying, recording or by any information storage and retrieval system, without permission in writing from authors and the publisher.

は じ め に

Fundamental English Grammar with Short Readings『読解力につなげるコア英文法』は英文法の基礎を理解し、英語コミュニケーション能力の向上を目的とした初級・中級学生のためのテキストです。

本書の特徴は内容が二部構成になっていることです。前半は基本英文法の解説とその練習問題です。後半は文法解説で扱った文法項目を含んだショートリーディングになっています。

文法解説で扱う英文法は英語を理解し活用するために重要でかつ必須の基本項目を精選しました。そして、文法内容を説明する例文は学習者の皆さんが無理なく理解できるシンプルなものになっています。短い例文ですのでぜひ繰り返し発音して理解を深めてください。また、例文の後にある◆では、特に留意すべき事項や間違えやすい事項を補足的に説明しています。そして、応用・発展的な内容を【研究】【参考】でコンパクトに解説しています。学習内容を深めるための参考にしてください。

練習問題は各ユニットで学んだ英文法の定着をはかるものです。文法解説とその練習問題は対応していますので、解らない問題があれば文法解説を参照してください。

ショートリーディングはオーストラリア出身のマーガレット先生の書き下ろしです。100語程度の短い読み物で、各ユニットに３つのショートリーディングがあります。それぞれにNotes（注）をつけましたので英文理解の参考にしてください。内容は芸術、アジアの国々の文化、身近な出来事、日本文化、工学、動物、気候問題、旅行、文学、日本人学生の生活、英語圏の文化、生き物、食べ物、高齢化問題などバラエティーに富んでいます。すべてのショートリーディングは各ユニットで扱った文法項目に対応する表現が含まれています。学生の皆さんが興味を持った内容があればインターネットなどで検索し内容理解を深めてください。

テキスト名の fundamental とは「基礎の」という意味の他「重要な、必須の」の意味も含みます。多くの学生が、英文法は苦手だけれども英語でのコミュニケーションには興味があると考えています。そのためにはやはり基本的な文法能力が必要です。本書ではそのために必要な重要かつ必須の文法項目を扱っています。本書でもう一度英文法の確認をすることで、皆さんの英語コミュニケーション能力の向上のお手伝いができればと願っています。

最後になりましたが、本書の製作にあたり朝日出版社の日比野忠氏に大変お世話になりました。この場をおかりして感謝いたします。

2018 年　豪雨と猛暑の夏
著者一同

Contents

はじめに

| Unit 1 | 名　詞 .... 2 |
| Short Readings .... 56 |

| Unit 2 | 冠　詞 .... 4 |
| Short Readings .... 57 |

| Unit 3 | 代名詞 (1) .... 6 |
| Short Readings .... 58 |

| Unit 4 | 代名詞 (2) .... 8 |
| Short Readings .... 59 |

| Unit 5 | 時　制 .... 10 |
| Short Readings .... 60 |

| Unit 6 | 進行形 .... 12 |
| Short Readings .... 61 |

| Unit 7 | 完了形 (1) .... 14 |
| Short Readings .... 62 |

| Unit 8 | 完了形 (2) .... 16 |
| Short Readings .... 63 |

| Unit 9 | 助動詞 (1) .... 18 |
| Short Readings .... 64 |

| Unit 10 | 助動詞 (2) .... 20 |
| Short Readings .... 65 |

| Unit 11 | 態 (1) .... 22 |
| Short Readings .... 66 |

| Unit 12 | 態 (2) .... 24 |
| Short Readings .... 67 |

| Unit 13 | 不定詞 (1) .... 26 |
| Short Readings .... 68 |

| Unit 14 | 不定詞 (2) .... 28 |
| Short Readings .... 69 |

| Unit 15 | 分詞 (1) .... 30 |
| Short Readings .... 70 |

| Unit 16 | 分詞 (2) .... 32 |
| Short Readings .... 71 |

| Unit 17 | 動名詞 (1) .... 34 |
| Short Readings .... 72 |

| Unit 18 | 動名詞 (2) .... 36 |
| Short Readings .... 73 |

| Unit 19 | 形容詞・副詞 .... 38 |
| Short Readings .... 74 |

| Unit 20 | 比　較 (1) .... 40 |
| Short Readings .... 75 |

| Unit 21 | 比　較 (2) .... 42 |
| Short Readings .... 76 |

| Unit 22 | 前置詞 .... 44 |
| Short Readings .... 77 |

| Unit 23 | 関係詞 (1) .... 46 |
| Short Readings .... 78 |

| Unit 24 | 関係詞 (2) .... 48 |
| Short Readings .... 79 |

| Unit 25 | 仮定法 (1) .... 50 |
| Short Readings .... 80 |

| Unit 26 | 仮定法 (2) .... 52 |
| Short Readings .... 81 |

Fundamental English Grammar
with Short Readings

Unit 1　名　詞

A　数えられる名詞

① **普通名詞** (boy, cat, desk, flower, river, week, *etc.*)：同種類のものに共通の名を表す名詞で、単数形と複数形とがある。

1. A **fox** is a cunning **animal**.
2. There is a **woman** at the **door**.

② **集合名詞** (class, family, audience, team, people, *etc.*)：人や物の集合体を表す名詞で、単数と複数の2通りに扱われる。

3. a. Her **family** *is* very large. 〈集合体〉
   b. Her **family** *are* all tall. 〈構成員〉
4. a. There *was* a small **audience**. 〈集合体〉
   b. The **audience** *were* all foreigners. 〈構成員〉

B　数えられない名詞

① **固有名詞** (Newton, Paris, Spain, Hyde Park, *etc.*)：特定の人・物・場所などを表す名詞で、必ず大文字で書きはじめる。

1. **Mr. Ford** teaches law at **Oxford**.
2. **Canberra** is the capital of **Australia**.

② **物質名詞** (milk, bread, sand, gold, fire, *etc.*)：一定の形がない物質や材料を表す名詞で、常に単数形で用いられる。

3. **Diamond** is a precious stone.
4. I want *two pieces of* **chalk**.　［◆ two chalks は不可］

☞その他：*a cup of* tea, *a sheet of* paper, *a cake of* soap, *a bottle of* beer, *a loaf of* bread, *a spoonful of* sugar, *etc.*

③ **抽象名詞** (beauty, love, kindness, success, advice, *etc.*)：性質・状態・行為などの抽象概念を表す名詞で、a, an をつけず、また複数形にもしない。

5. A heart shape is the symbol of **love**.
6. He gave me good **advice**.　［◆「1つの助言」は *a piece of* **advice**］

C　名詞の転用 — 数えられない名詞が普通名詞として用いられることがある。

1. I want *an* evening **paper**.「新聞」 〈物質名詞→普通名詞〉
2. There are *three* **Yamadas** in our class.「山田という名の生徒」
   〈固有名詞→普通名詞〉
3. The show was *a* great **success**.「成功した事」 〈抽象名詞→普通名詞〉

EXERCISE 1

I 次の各文中の、下線を引いた名詞の種類を言いなさい。

1. This is a <u>poem</u> of great <u>beauty</u>. (　　　) (　　　)
2. Were there many <u>people</u> at the <u>party</u>? (　　　) (　　　)
3. <u>Diligence</u> is the key to <u>success</u>. (　　　) (　　　)
4. <u>Bob</u> is a member of the basketball <u>team</u>. (　　　) (　　　)
5. I put two spoonfuls of <u>sugar</u> in your <u>coffee</u>. (　　　) (　　　)

II 次の各文の（　）内から適切なものを選びなさい。

1. I like (a pear / pears) very much.
2. The bridge is built of (stone / stones).
3. Our class (is / are) all present today.
4. Two (family / families) live in this one house.

III 次の各文の下線部の誤りを正しなさい。

1. My uncle gave me <u>an advice</u>.

2. I want <u>two yellow chalks</u>.

3. She bought <u>three wines</u> at King's Mart.

IV 次の各文の意味を書きなさい。

1. Our chemistry teacher wears glasses.

2. I don't believe in life after death.

3. The cross is the symbol of Christianity.

V 次の各文の（　）内の語を並べかえて意味の通る文にしなさい。

1. She (a / of / brought / glass / water / me).

2. I (two / yesterday / of / bought / bread / loaves).

3. He (juice / a / breakfast / glass / drinks / with / of).

Unit 2　冠　詞

A　不定冠詞の用法 ― a, an は数えられる名詞の単数形の前につける。
① ばく然と1つのものをさす。
　1. Betty was wearing **a** green blouse.
② 「1つの」(= one) の意味を表す。
　2. He will be back in **a** day or two.
③ 種類全体を表す。「～というもの」
　3. **An** owl can see in the dark.《口語》［◆ The owl... は文語］
④ 「～につき」(= per) の意味を表す。
　4. He goes fishing once **a** month.
⑤ 「ある」(= a certain) の意味を表す。
　5. **A** young man called on me this morning.

B　定冠詞の用法 ― the はどんな名詞にも、また単複の区別なく用いられる。
① 前に一度出た名詞をくり返す。
　1. He has a daughter. **The** daughter is a nurse.
② 周囲の状況から明らかな場合。
　2. Look at **the** blackboard.
③ たった1つのものをさす。
　3. **The** sun rises in **the** east.
④ 句や節によって限定されているものに用いる。
　4. **The** legs *of the table* are long.
　5. This is **the** jacket *I wanted to buy*.
⑤ 種類全体を表す。「～というもの」
　6. **The** cow is a useful animal.　　［◆ **Cows** are useful animals. は口語］
⑥ 〈the＋形容詞〉で「…の人々」の意味を表す。
　7. **The** *young* should help **the** *old*.
⑦ 〈by the＋名詞〉で「～につき」の意味を表す。
　8. You can rent a boat *by* **the** *hour*.

C　冠詞の省略
　1. **Doctor**, come here please.　　　〈呼びかけ〉
　2. **Father** is out, but **mother** is in.　〈家族関係〉
　3. We go to **church** every Sunday.　〈建物などが本来の目的を表す場合〉
　4. They elected him **President**.　　〈官職・身分を表す語が補語となる場合〉

EXERCISE 2

I 次の各文の（ ）内に、必要に応じて適切な冠詞を入れなさい。不必要なところには×印をつけなさい。

1. Please turn on (　　) air conditioner.
2. What time does (　　) school begin?
3. This is (　　) dress I bought last week.
4. Mr. Tanaka is (　　) teacher at our school.
5. (　　) cheeze is sold by (　　) pound.
6. There was not (　　) cloud in (　　) sky.
7. I saw a man by the gate. (　　) man had (　　) video camera in his hand.

II 次の各文の適切な位置に冠詞を補って文を完成しなさい。

1. Juice in bottle is fresh.

2. Earth moves around sun.

3. There is world map on wall.

4. You can rent bicycle by day.

III 次の各文の意味を書きなさい。

1. Art is, in a sense, harmony.

2. We voted him captain of the football team.

3. The poor are sometimes happier than the rich.

IV 次の各文の（ ）内の語を並べかえて意味の通る文にしなさい。

1. I (these / a / take / twice / day / tablets).

2. He (just / the / went / barbershop / now / to).

3. This (my / arrives / time / is / plane / when / the).

Unit 3　代名詞（1）

A 「一般の人々」を表す we, you, they

1. **We** should be kind to others.　「人は、われわれは」
2. **You** can't trust him.　「人は」　［◆we より口語的］
3. **They** say that she is an able teacher.

it の特別用法

1. **It**'s half past four by my watch.　　　　　　　　　　〈時間〉
2. **It** will be windy at sea today.　　　　　　　　　　　〈天候〉
3. How far is **it** to the nearest bus stop?　　　　　　　〈距離〉
4. In winter **it** gets dark at five.　　　　　　　　　　　〈明暗〉
5. **It** is not good *to eat between meals*.　　　　　　　〈形式主語〉
6. I found **it** impossible *to persuade him*.　　　　　　〈形式目的語〉
7. **It** was yesterday *that I got his letter*.　　　　　　　〈強調構文〉

B this と that

① 直接に物をさす場合：this は近いもの、that は遠いものをさす。

1. **This** is a desk and **that** is a table.
2. **These** are my pens and **those** are Joe's.
   【参考】 this, that は人にも用いられる：Who is **this**?「こちらは…」/ Is that〔《米》**this**〕Mr. White?「(電話で) そちらは…」

② 名詞のくり返しを避ける場合

3. The *climate* here is like **that** in Italy.
4. Her *manners* are **those** of a polite girl.

③ 前述（または後述）の文の内容をさす場合

5. *He said nothing,* and **that** made her angry.　　　〈前述の文の内容〉
6. Answer me **this**. *Where were you last night?*　　〈後述の文の内容〉

C 再帰代名詞 ― 語尾が -self, -selves で終わる代名詞という。

① 再帰用法：動詞・前置詞の目的語となる。

1. The boy hid **himself** behind a tree.　「かくれた」
2. The cat is licking **itself** with its tongue.

② 強意用法：名詞・代名詞とともに用いて、それらの意味を強調する。

3. I spoke to the president **himself**.　「社長本人」
4. She cooked the fish **herself**.　「自分で」

Fundamental English Grammar

EXERCISE 3

I 次の各文中の it が何を表しているか指摘しなさい。

1. What time is it? — It's ten past nine. (　　　)
2. It was last Sunday that I heard the news. (　　　)
3. Where is the diary? Have you seen it? (　　　)
4. It is difficult to find a four-leaf clover. (　　　)

II 次の各文の ( ) 内に、we, you, they, this, that のうち適切なものを入れなさい。

1. (　　　) drink a lot of beer in Germany.
2. Do (　　　) eat beef in your country?
3. I know (　　　): he is my strong rival.
4. (　　　) have many rainy days in June.
5. His behavior is (　　　) of a gentleman.

III 次の各文の ( ) 内に適切な再帰代名詞を入れなさい。

1. He looked at (　　　) in the mirror.
2. We must take good care of (　　　).
3. The girl hid (　　　) in the closet.
4. I enjoyed (　　　) at the party last night.

IV 次の各文の意味を書きなさい。

1. Peggy dressed herself quickly and went out.

2. Old Mr. Todd was as gentle as a lamb.

3. It is certain that he will win the Nobel prize.

V 次の各文の ( ) 内の語を並べかえて意味の通る文にしなさい。

1. They (that / up / will / say / go / prices).

2. Judy (call / himself / the / to / principal / decided).

3. He (it / to / the / difficult / machine / found / use).

Unit 4　代名詞（2）

A 再帰代名詞を含む慣用表現
1. I walked in the woods **by myself**.「ひとりで」(＝alone)
2. You must think **for yourself**.「自分で；自分のために」
3. Human nature is not gentle **in itself**.「それ自体では、元来」

B 不定代名詞 — 不特定の人や物、数量を表す代名詞をいい、その多くは形容詞としても用いられる。不定代名詞と動詞の数（すう）に注意。

① **one**
1. **One** must do one's [his] duty.《文語》　　　　　　〈一般の人々〉
2. If you want a cake, I'll give you **one**. (＝a cake).　〈不特定の物〉
　　Cf. If you want this cake, I'll give **it** to you.　　〈特定の物〉

② **some, any**：some は肯定文に、any は疑問文・否定文・条件文に用いる。
3. Do you have **any** butter? Yes, I have **some**.
4. If you have **any** questions, please ask them now.
　【参考】勧誘や依頼を表すときは、疑問文でも some を用いる：Will you buy me **some** stamps? (＝Please buy me some stamps.)

③ **other, another**
5. One suit is big, and **the other** is small.　　　　　〈もう一方の物〉
6. This glass isn't clean. Please give me **another**.　〈別の1つ〉

④ **both**：「両方とも」の意味で、複数扱い。
7. **Both** of them *were* very hungry.
8. **Both** (the) women *are* hairdressers.

⑤ **each**：「めいめい（の）」の意味で、単数扱い。
9. **Each** of us *is* in the same grade.
10. **Each** student *has* his own study room.

⑥ **every**：「すべての」の意味で、単数扱い。
11. **Every** bird *has* its wings.
　　Cf. **All** birds *have* their wings.

⑦ **either**：「どちらか一方」「どちらの…も」の意味で、単数扱い。
12. **Either** of the two answers *is* wrong.
13. You can park on **either** side of the road.　「道路の両側に」

⑧ **neither**：「どちら（の…）も～ない」の意味で、単数扱い。
14. **Neither** of the pictures *was* [*were*] sold.　[◆口語では複数扱い]
15. **Neither** window *faces* the lake.

EXERCISE 4

I 次の各文の（ ）内から適切なものを選びなさい。
1. All the grapes in the box (was / were) rotten.
2. I gave a toy to (each / every) of the children.
3. (Both / Either) of them are fond of ice cream.
4. I have lost my eraser. I must buy (one / it).

II 次の各文の（ ）内に、下記の語群から適切な語を選んで入れなさい。
1. (　　　) man has his weak points.
2. One is black and the (　　　) is white.
3. I like (　　　) of these pictures.
4. Is there (　　　) sugar left in the bowl?
5. There are trees on (　　　) side of the street.

　　　[any / either / every / neither / other]

III 日本文の意味を表すように、次の各文の（ ）内に適切な語を入れなさい。
1. 彼女はひとりで行くのをこわがっている。
　　She is afraid to go (　　　) (　　　).
2. 競争は本来悪いことではない。
　　Competition is not a bad thing (　　　) (　　　).

IV 次の各文の意味を書きなさい。
1. Neither of us has been to Europe before.

2. You may choose either of the two sweets.

3. Bill fell from the ladder and hurt himself.

V 次の各文の（ ）内の語を並べかえて意味の通る文にしなさい。
1. Each (in / box / peaches / has / it / twenty).

2. Both (are / of / fans / brothers / soccer / my).

3. One (at / must / ID / door / one's / the / show).

Unit 5　時　制

「時」を表す動詞の形を**時制**という。英語には次のような3つの時制がある。

A　現在時制の用法

① 現在の事実・状態を表す。
　1. Tom Brown **is** a famous actor.
　2. His house **stands** on the hill.

② 現在の習慣的動作を表す。
　3. I **get** up at six every morning.

③ 一般的事実・不変の真理を表す。
　4. Five and six **make(s)** eleven.

④ 確定的な未来の予定を表す。
　5. We **have** a dinner party next Saturday.

　【研究】時や条件を表す副詞節では、未来のことを述べる場合でも現在時制が用いられる：I'll tell him so when he **comes**.〈副詞節〉／
　　　　　I don't know when he **will come**.〈名詞節〉

B　過去時制の用法

① 過去の動作・状態を表す。
　1. We **talked** about classical music last night.
　2. He **had** a fine villa by the lake.

② 過去の習慣的動作を表す。
　3. We **went** to the seaside every summer.

C　未来時制の用法

① 単純未来：主語や話し手の意志を含まない、単なる未来をいう。
　1. I **will** [**shall**] be 20 years old in May.　［◆ shall はおもに《米》］

② 意志未来：平叙文（事実を述べる文）では主語や話し手の意志を表し、疑問文では聞き手の意志をたずねるのに用いられる。
　　(a) 主語の意志を表す場合
　2. I **will** tell you about my childhood.　「〜しましょう」
　3. This wood **won't** burn.　「どうしても〜しない」[won't＝will not]
　　(b) 聞き手の意志をたずねる場合
　4. **Shall** I sing a song for you?　「〜しましょうか」
　5. **Will** you lend me your ball-point pen?　「〜してくれませんか」

EXERCISE 5

I 次の各文の現在時制の用法が、左ページの ①〜④ のどれにあたるか指摘しなさい。

1. He often quarrels with his wife.   (   )
2. Fukuyama lies east of Hiroshima.   (   )
3. Water consists of hydrogen and oxygen.   (   )
4. We go to the seaside every summer.   (   )
5. We leave for Brazil on Monday morning.   (   )

II 次の各文の (　) 内の動詞を適切な形に変えなさい。

1. Henry (be) at the supermarket then.   (   )
2. She will not come if it (rain) tomorrow.   (   )
3. I (learn) dancing when I was in Spain.   (   )
4. The Danube (run) through the middle of Budapest.   (   )

III 次の各文の (　) 内に will または shall を入れなさい。

1. (   ) you pass me the salt?
2. What time (   ) we meet tomorrow?
3. (   ) I show you around the city?
4. It (   ) get cloudy in the afternoon.

IV 次の各文の意味を書きなさい。

1. I sometimes spend the weekend in Hakone.

2. The summer vacation begins on August 2nd.

3. He took his daughter to the doctor yesterday.

V 次の各文の (　) 内の語を並べかえて意味の通る文にしなさい。

1. He (that / won't / his / says / work / son).

2. I (you / story / tell / interesting / will / an).

3. Will (it / this / you / to / evening / fax / me)?

Unit 6 進行形

A 現在進行形 (am [are, is] ＋ 〜ing)

① 現在進行中の動作を表す。 「〜している、しつつある」
  1. I **am reading** a comic book.
  2. He **is writing** a composition.

② 現在の反復的動作を表す。always, constantly, all the time などの副詞（句）を伴って用いられ、話し手の驚き、いらだち、非難などの気持ちを含むことが多い。 「いつも［たえず、しょっちゅう］〜している」
  3. Fashion **is** *constantly* **changing**. 〈驚きの表現〉
  4. You **are** *always* **leaving** the door open. 〈非難の表現〉

③ 近い未来の予定を表す。おもに往来・発着を表す動詞 (go, come, leave, arrive, *etc.*) が用いられる。 「〜するつもりだ、〜する予定だ」
  5. When **is** she **coming** to Seattle again?
  6. We **are leaving** for Hawaii next Monday.

B 過去進行形 (was [were] ＋ 〜ing) ─ 時制が過去になる点を除いて、現在進行形と用法は同じである。 「(いつも) 〜していた」
  1. When he came, I **was doing** my homework. 〈過去の進行中の動作〉
  2. She **was** *always* **finding** fault with him. 〈過去の反復的動作〉

C 未来進行形 (will [shall] be ＋ 〜ing)

① 未来の進行中の動作を表す。 「〜しているだろう」
  1. It **will be raining** tomorrow morning.

② 近い未来の予定を表す。 「〜するだろう、〜することになるだろう」
  2. My mother **will be coming** home soon.

D ふつう進行形をとらない動詞

① 知覚動詞：see, hear, feel, smell, taste, *etc.*
  1. Lilies **smell** sweet.
  2. This sauce **tastes** strange.

② 状態動詞：be, have, know, love, think, resemble, belong to, *etc.*
  3. Cathy **resembles** her brother.
  4. They **belong to** the yacht club.

  【研究】 状態動詞も意味によっては進行形にすることがある：She **has** blue eyes and blonde hair. / He is **having** lunch with Bob.

EXERCISE 6

I 次の各文の（ ）内の動詞を現在、過去、未来のいずれかの進行形に変えなさい。

1. She (listen) to music this morning.　　　　　　（　　　　　）
2. I (wait) for you at ten tomorrow morning.　　　（　　　　　）
3. Take an umbrella. It (rain) outside.　　　　　　（　　　　　）
4. I heard a loud noise when I (drink) tea.　　　　（　　　　　）
5. Next week they (travel) around Hokkaido.　　　（　　　　　）
6. My mother is busy now. She (clean) the room.　（　　　　　）

II 次の各文の（ ）内に入れるのに最も適切なものを(a)〜(c)から選び、その記号で答えなさい。

1. Look! A white cat (　　　) by the door.
   (a) is sitting　(b) was sitting　(c) sits
2. He fell down while he (　　　) after the dog.
   (a) is running　(b) was running　(c) ran
3. This wine (　　　) like strawberries.
   (a) is smelling　(b) was smelling　(c) smells
4. At this time tomorrow she (　　　) in Shinjuku.
   (a) is shopping　(b) was shopping　(c) will be shopping

III 次の各文の下線部の誤りを正しなさい。

1. I <u>cooked</u> dinner at that time.

2. My grandmother <u>still lives</u>.

3. This brooch <u>is belonging</u> to her.

IV 次の各文の（ ）内の語を並べかえて意味の通る文にしなさい。

1. I (be / tomorrow / my / will / sister / helping).

2. He (about / always / food / is / the / complaining).

3. I (going / business / Sendai / am / on / tomorrow / to).

Unit 7　完了形（1）

A 現在完了形（have [has] ＋過去分詞）— 過去の動作・状態が現在となんらかの意味でつながりがあることを示す。

① 動作の完了・動作の結果：just, already, yet, recently などの副詞を伴うことが多い。「ちょうど［すでに］〜してしまった」「〜してしまって（今は）〜だ」

1. I **have** *just* **finished** my homework.
2. She **has gone** to the convenience store.

   【参考】2 は「彼女はコンビニへ行って、今はここにいない」を意味する。これに反し、She went to the convenience store. は「彼女はコンビニへ行った」という事実を述べているだけで、今もコンビニいるのか、それともコンビニから帰ってきたのかは不明。

② 現在までの経験：ever, never, before, once, twice などの副詞を伴うことが多い。「〜したことがある［ない］」

3. **Have** you *ever* **ridden** in a helicopter?
4. I **have** *never* **seen** such a beautiful sunset.

   【研究】have been to ... は、「…へ行ったことがある」と「…へ行ってきたところだ」という 2 通りの意味に用いられる：I **have been to** Osaka by bus twice. / I **have** *just* **been** to Haneda Airport to meet my uncle.

③ 現在までの状態の継続を表す。

5. I **have known** Mr. Smith *for seven years*.
6. I **have been** busy *all morning*.　「朝からずっと…」

   【注意】現在完了形は、明らかに過去を示す語句 (yesterday, last week, two days ago, *etc*.) や疑問副詞 when とともに用いることはできない：When **did** he **go** out?［正］/ When **has** he **gone** out?［誤］

B 現在完了進行形 (have [has] been〜ing) — 現在までの動作の継続を表す。for..., since..., how long などの副詞句を伴うことが多い。「…の間［以来］〜している［してきた］」

1. I **have been studying** German *for six years*.
2. It **has been snowing** *since last night*.
3. How *long* **have** you **been teaching** mathematics?

   【参考】1 とほぼ同義の I **have studied** German *for six years*. は、「私はドイツ語を 6 年間勉強したことがある」という意味にもとれる。

EXERCISE 7

I 次の各文の（ ）内の動詞を現在完了形か現在完了進行形に変えなさい。
1. They (play) golf since early this morning. (　　　　)
2. He (not have) breakfast yet. (　　　　)
3. The child (sleep) for five hours. (　　　　)
4. I (meet) her in Boston three times. (　　　　)
5. Mary (be) in hospital for two weeks. (　　　　)

II 日本文の意味を表すように、次の各文の（ ）内に適切な語を入れなさい。
1. あなたはユーフォーを見たことがありますか。
   (　　) you ever (　　) a UFO?
2. 雨が2日間降り続いている。
   It (　　) (　　) (　　) for two days.

III 次の各文の下線部の誤りを正しなさい。
1. I <u>live</u> in Fukuoka for five years.

2. It <u>has been</u> very cold last winter.

3. The train <u>has left</u> ten minutes ago.

IV 次の各文の意味を書きなさい。
1. She has been taking violin lessons since last year.

2. I haven't heard from him since he went to Kenya.

3. I have just been to Ueno Station to see a friend off.

V 次の各文の（ ）内の語を並べかえて意味の通る文にしなさい。
1. She (last / been / since / week / here / has).

2. He (yet / from / hasn't / his / returned / journey).

3. I (such / never / picture / have / a / seen / beautiful).

Unit 8　完了形（2）

A　**過去完了形（had + 過去分詞）** ── 過去のある時までの完了・経験・継続を表す。
それぞれの用法については現在完了形に準じて考えればよい。

① 過去のある時までの動作の完了を表す。
「（その時までには）もう〜してしまっていた」

1. I **had** *just* **written** a letter when he came back.
2. The train **had** *already* **left** when I got to the station.

② 過去のある時までの経験を表す。
「（その時までに）〜したことがあった［なかった］」

3. He asked me if I **had** *ever* **seen** a koala.
4. I **had** *never* **been** abroad before I was fifty.

③ 過去のある時までの状態の継続を表す。
「（その時まで）ずっと〜だった［〜していた］」

5. I **had known** about Mrs. Jones before I met her.
6. He said that the house **had been** empty *for a month*.

B　**過去完了進行形 (had been + 〜ing)** ── 過去のある時までの動作の継続を表す。
「その時まで［その時より前から］ずっと〜していた」

1. We **had been dating** until we broke up last year.
2. We **had been talking** about Ted when he entered the room.
   Cf. We **were talking** about Ted when he entered the room.
   [◆「部屋に入って来る」というテッドの動作と、「テッドのうわさ話をする」という私たちの動作が同時に行われていた場合]

C　**未来完了形 (will [shall] have + 過去分詞)**

① 未来のある時までの動作の完了を表す。
「（その時（まで）には）〜してしまっているだろう」

1. They **will have arrived** in Seoul *by five o'clock*.

② 未来のある時までの経験を表す。
「（その時（まで）には）〜したことになるだろう」

2. If I see the film again, I **will have seen** it *three times*.

③ 未来のある時までの継続を表す。
「（その時まで）ずっと〜していたことになるだろう」

3. On June 10 we **will have been married** *for 25 years*.
   「6月10日で私たちは結婚してから25年たったことになる」

EXERCISE 8

I 次の各文の（　）内の動詞を過去完了形か過去完了進行形に変えなさい。

1. We (play) chess for an hour when he came.　（　　　　　）
2. She said that she (never see) a rainbow.　（　　　　　）
3. The concert (already begin) when I arrived.　（　　　　　）
4. I (stay) in Rome before I came back to Japan.　（　　　　　）

II 次の各文の（　）内の動詞を未来完了形に変えなさい。

1. She (move) by the end of this month.　（　　　　　）
2. I (buy) a new smartphone by next Wednesday.　（　　　　　）
3. Next July we (live) in Chicago for 15 years.　（　　　　　）

III 次の各文の下線部の誤りを正しなさい。

1. I asked her when she <u>met</u> Mrs. Yokoyama.

2. He <u>was</u> ill for a month when I visited him.

3. I <u>have ever climb</u> Mt. Fuji before. This is my first time.

IV 次の各文の意味を書きなさい。

1. My father had already left home when I got up.

2. Her eyes were red because she had been crying.

3. All the marigolds in my garden will have died by next week.

4. I recognized Mr. Smith at once, for I had often seen him.

V 次の各文の（　）内の語を並べかえて意味の通る文にしなさい。

1. By next week (have / we / to / will / moved / Okayama).

2. (been / the / I / piano / had / playing) until that time.

3. She said (to / had / that / been / Germany / she / never).

Unit 9　助動詞（1）

A　can の用法

① 能力：「〜することができる」
  1. He **can** speak Spanish fluently.
  2. My sister **can't** ride a bicycle.
     【研究】can の代わりに be able to もよく用いられる。とくに未来形は will can とはならず、will be able to を用いる。

② 許可：「〜してもよい」《口語》
  3. **Can** (＝May) I smoke in here? ［◆May のほうがていねいな表現］

③ 推量：疑問文で「いったい〜だろうか」、否定文で「…のはずがない」
  4. **Can** the rumor be true?
  5. He **cannot** be a lazy fellow.

B　may の用法

① 許可：「〜してもよい」
  1. **May** I park my car here?
     — Yes, you **may**. / No, you **may [must] not**.
     【注意】may not は「不許可」を、must not は「強い禁止」を表す。これらの答えは目下以外の人に対しては失礼なので、Yes, certainly.（ええ、いいですよ）/ I'm sorry you can't.（すみませんが、駐車できません）などを用いるのがふつう。

② 推量：「〜かもしれない」
  2. She **may** come at any moment.
  3. He **may not** know the truth.

③ 祈願：「〜しますように」《文語》
  4. **May** you live long!　［◆Long **may** you live! とも言う］

C　must の用法

① 必要・義務：「〜しなければならない」
  1. **Must** I take this coat with me?
     — Yes, you **must**. / No, you **needn't [don't have to]**.
     【研究】must の代わりに have to もよく用いられる。過去形には had to を、未来形には will have to を用いる。

② 肯定的推量：「〜にちがいない」
  2. Her grandfather **must** be about seventy.

Fundamental English Grammar

EXERCISE 9

I 次の各文の（　）内に、can, may, must のうち適切なものを入れなさい。

1. (　　　) you have a pleasant trip!
2. He (　　　) play the flute very well.
3. (　　　) he really be a policeman?
4. You (　　　) fill out the form with a pen.
5. (　　　) I help him? — No, you don't have to.

II 日本文の意味を表すように、次の各文の（　）内に適切な語を入れなさい。

1. あなたがいつも幸せでありますように。
   (　　　) you always (　　　) happy!
2. 私たちはその朝早く出発しなければならなかった。
   We (　　　) (　　　) start early that morning.

III 次の各文の下線部の誤りを正しなさい。

1. You <u>will can ski</u> very well soon.

2. You <u>will must sign</u> your letter.

3. That <u>may not be</u> Mr. Takagi; he's in Kyoto.

IV 次の各文の意味を書きなさい。

1. Nobody can leave the country without a passport.

2. You may go out, but you must come home before dark.

3. You must not cross the road; the light is still red.

V 次の各文の（　）内の語を並べかえて意味の通る文にしなさい。

1. May (go / a / I / tomorrow / for / drive)?

2. He (over / old / must / seventy / be / years).

3. You (wash / meals / your / before / must / hands).

Unit 10　助動詞（2）

A　would の用法

① 過去の習慣：「（よく）〜したものだった」　[◆不規則な習慣を表す]
  1. Uncle John **would** sit there all day.
② 過去の拒絶：「どうしても〜しなかった」
  2. She **wouldn't** take the medicine. [wouldn't＝would not]
③ ていねいな表現：「〜してくださいませんか」
  3. **Would** you help me with my work?

B　should の用法

① 義務・当然：「〜すべきである」　[◆must より意味が弱い]
  1. You **should** see a doctor at once.
  2. You **should not** speak so loud.
② 感情・判断・命令・助言・提案などを表す動詞に続く **that** 節で
  3. It is quite natural that you **should** feel nervous.
  4. It is necessary that you **should** keep your promise.
  5. The doctor advised that I **(should)** take more exercise.
  6. He suggested that we **(should)** go in his car.
   【注意】5, 6 の場合、《米》では動詞の原形だけを用いることが多い。

C　ought to の用法：「〜すべきである」　[◆should より意味が強い]

  1. You **ought to** be ashamed of yourself.
  2. You **ought not to** neglect your duty.

D　used to の用法

① 過去の習慣：「〜するのが常だった」　[◆規則的な習慣を表す]
  1. I **used to** take a walk every morning.　「今はしないが…」
② 過去の状態：「以前は〜だった」
  2. There **used to** be a pond around here.　「今はないが…」

E　「助動詞＋have＋過去分詞」の用法

  1. The old man **may have lost** his way.　「〜したかもしれない」
  2. He **must have failed** the job interview.　「〜したにちがいない」
  3. She **cannot have stolen** your handbag.　「〜したはずがない」
  4. You **should [ought to] have met** him there.　「〜すべきだったのに」

EXERCISE 10

I 次の各文の ( ) 内から適切なものを選びなさい。

1. (Would / Should) you come with me, please?
2. You (would / should) wear your seat belt.
3. It is natural that a baby (would / should) cry.
4. He (would / should) sit up till late at night.
5. The teacher ordered that they (would / should) be silent.

II 次の各組の文がほぼ同じ意味になるように、( ) 内に適切な語を入れなさい。

1. We once lived in New York.
   We (　　) (　　) live in New York.
2. I am sorry you didn't water the plants.
   You (　　) (　　) have watered the plants.

III 次の各文の下線部の誤りを正しなさい。

1. You ought to not be cruel to animals.

2. He may be at the post office then.

3. It is strange that we would meet here.

IV 次の各文の意味を書きなさい。

1. He insisted that his son should go to college.

2. It is important that you should learn to read.

3. I used to ride a minibike when I was a student.

V 次の各文の ( ) 内の語を並べかえて意味の通る文にしなさい。

1. We (sit / that / to / under / and / used / tree / talk).

2. She (her / not / advice / take / would / father's).

3. He (have / thing / said / a / cannot / foolish / such).

Unit 11　態（１）

A 能動態と受動態 ― 動作を行うものを主語にした動詞の形を**能動態**、動作を他から受けるものを主語にした形を**受動態**という。

B 受動態のつくり方

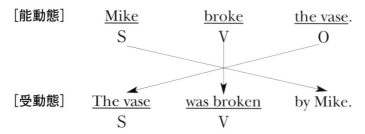

① 能動態の文の目的語（O）を主語（S）にする。
② 動詞（V）を「be＋過去分詞」の形に変える。
③ 能動態の主語を「by＋(代)名詞」の形にして、文尾に置く。
④ 次のような場合には、ふつう「by＋(代)名詞」は表されない。
　1. This insect **is called** a cicada.　　　　〈動作主が一般の人々〉
　2. He **was killed** in battle.「戦死した」　〈動作主が不明〉

C 受動態の基本形

① 「主語＋動詞＋目的語」の受動態
　1. a. Bell **invented** the telephone.　(the telephone＝目的語)
　　 b. The telephone **was invented** by Bell.

② 「主語＋動詞＋間接目的語＋直接目的語」の受動態
　2. a. He **gave** me this doll.　(me＝間接目的語、this doll＝直接目的語)
　　 b. I **was given** this doll by him.　[◆ a の受動態は b がふつう]
　　 c. This doll **was given** (to) me by him.
　【研究】 c では me の代わりに名詞が用いられると、to が必要になる：
　　　　This doll was given to Linda by him.

③ 「主語＋動詞＋目的語＋補語」の受動態
　3. a. She **keeps** the room clean.　(the room＝目的語、clean＝補語)
　　 b. The room **is kept** clean by her.

④ 否定文・疑問文の受動態
　4. This soup **was not made** by my sister.
　5. **Was** this soup **made** by your sister?

EXERCISE 11

I 次の各文を受動態に書きかえなさい。

1. My aunt gave me this necklace.

2. We do not use this room now.

3. Her parents named her Harriet.

4. They sell old DVDs at that store.

II 次の各文を能動態に書きかえなさい。

1. Is Russian taught at that school?

2. She is loved by her grandchildren.

3. I was asked the way by a stranger.

4. The wall was painted white by my brother.

III 次の各文の意味を書きなさい。

1. A camel is called the ship of the desert.

2. English is spoken in many parts of the world.

3. He was appointed chairperson of the committee.

IV 次の各文の ( ) 内の語を並べかえて意味の通る文にしなさい。

1. The cat (found / a / dead / in / was / ditch).

2. A long letter (me / was / Jack / sent / by / to).

3. The cake (her / by / made / friends / was / Jenny / for).

Unit 12　態（2）

A　注意すべき受動態

① **who** で始まる疑問文の受動態
1. a. *Who* **painted** this picture?
   b. *By whom* **was** this picture **painted**?　《文語》
   c. *Who* **was** this picture **painted** *by*?　《口語》

② 助動詞を含む場合の受動態
2. a. We **can see** the Tokyo Sky Tree from here.
   b. The Tokyo Sky Tree **can be seen** from here.

③ 完了形の受動態
3. a. Susan **has written** all those poems.
   b. All those poems **have been written** by Susan.

④ 進行形の受動態
4. a. The students **are discussing** the problem.
   b. The problem **is being discussed** by the students.

⑤ 群動詞の受動態
5. a. All the people **laughed at** him.
   b. He **was laughed at** by all the people.

⑥ **They say that** の受動態
6. a. **They say that** he is a famous magician.　「～だそうだ」
   b. **It is said that** he is a famous magician.
   c. He **is said to** be a famous magician.

B　by 以外の前置詞を用いる受動態

1. We **were** very **surprised at** the news.　「～に驚いた」
2. I **am pleased with** my exam results.　「～が気に入っている」
3. The sidewalk **is covered with** snow.　「～におおわれている」
4. He **is known to** everybody as a comedian.　「～に知られている」
5. I **am interested in** American literature.　「～に興味がある」

C　受動態のもつ2つの意味

1. The gate **was shut** at six yesterday.　「しめられた」　〈動作〉
2. The door **was shut** when I got there.　「しまっていた」　〈状態〉

【研究】動作の意味を強調するために、「get＋過去分詞」が用いられることもある：
He **got stung** by a bee.　「みつバチに刺された」

Fundamental English Grammar

EXERCISE 12

I 次の各文の態を変えなさい。

1. Who made this model airplane?

2. Love cannot be bought with money.

3. An old man spoke to me at the station.

4. All the cookies have been eaten by Jason.

II 次の各組の b が a の受動態になるように、（ ）内に適切な語を入れなさい。

1. a. You must carry this bag upstairs.
   b. This bag (　　) (　　) (　　) upstairs.
2. a. They are building a drugstore near here.
   b. A drugstore (　　) (　　) (　　) near here.
3. a. His lecture interested me very much.
   b. I (　　) very much (　　) (　　) his lecture.
4. a. The workers have repaired the house.
   b. The house (　　) (　　) (　　) by the workers.

III 次の各文の意味を書きなさい。

1. The top of the mountain is covered with snow.

2. He is known to everybody as an opera singer.

3. Mary is very pleased with her son's birthday present.

4. A speech is being made in the city hall by the mayor.

IV 次の各文の（ ）内の語を並べかえて意味の通る文にしなさい。

1. I (blunt / was / his / surprised / answer / at).

2. What (in / this / called / French / is / bird)?

3. He (to / a / said / painter / be / is / famous).

態（2）　25

Unit 13　不定詞（1）

「to＋動詞の原形」の形で、名詞・形容詞・副詞の働きをする。

A　名詞用法

① 「〜すること」という意味を表し、文中で、主語・補語・目的語として用いられる。

1. **To raise** chickens is not easy.　　　　　　　　　　　　〈主語〉
   【注意】不定詞が主語となる場合は、形式主語の it を文頭に立てることが多い：
   　　　It is not easy **to raise** chickens.
2. His plan is **to open** an Indian restaurant.　　　　　　　〈補語〉
3. I want **to get** a job as a sales clerk.　　　　　　　　　〈目的語〉
   【研究】不定詞の否定形は、not や never を to の前に置く：
   　　　He told us *not* **to make** so much noise.

② how や what などの疑問詞とともに用いられて、「どのようにして〜したらよいか」「何を〜したらよいか」などの意味を表す。

4. I taught him **how to bake** bread.
5. He didn't know **what to say**.
6. She asked me **which bus to take**.

B　形容詞用法 ── 不定詞が名詞・代名詞を後ろから修飾し、「〜すべき」「〜する（ための）」という意味を表す。

1. He isn't a *man* **to betray** his friends.
2. This is the best *way* **to cure** a cold.
3. Will you give me *something* **to drink**?
   【研究】不定詞に導かれた句の後に前置詞が置かれ、全体として（代）名詞を修飾することがある：There was no *chair* **to sit on**. この文の場合、on がないと「座る」という行為と「いす」とが無関係になってしまって、まずい。

C　副詞用法 ── 文中で副詞としての、いろいろな働きをする。

1. He went to France **to learn** painting.　「〜するために」　〈目的〉
2. I am very pleased **to see** you here.　「〜して」　　　　　〈原因〉
3. You are foolish **to lend** him money.　「〜するとは」　　〈理由〉
4. She grew up **to be** a great actress.　「…して〜になる」　〈結果〉
5. My grandfather is hard **to please**.　「〜するのに」　　　〈限定〉

EXERCISE 13

I 次の各文の下線部と同じ用法を含む文を、下から選びなさい。
1. He showed me <u>how to</u> fly a drone. (　　)
2. I want <u>to get</u> a job as a taxi driver. (　　)
3. My ambition is <u>to become</u> a diplomat. (　　)
4. He was the first man <u>to raise</u> his hand. (　　)
   (a) Paul doesn't like to read in bed.
   (b) I had nothing to do that afternoon.
   (c) My plan is to build a hotel there.
   (d) She asked me where to change trains.

II 日本文の意味を表すように、次の各文の ( ) 内に適切な語を入れなさい。
1. イタリア語は発音しやすい。
   Italian is (　　　) (　　　) pronounce.
2. 彼は成長して大詩人になった。
   He grew up (　　　) (　　　) a great poet.
3. 私は彼女に何をパーティーにもっていったらよいかと聞いた。
   I asked her (　　　) (　　　) (　　　) to the party.
4. 私は二度と遅刻するまいと心に決めた。
   I decided (　　　) (　　　) (　　　) late again.

III 次の各文の意味を書きなさい。
1. This apron has no pockets to put things in.

2. Our neighbors told us where to go shopping.

3. You are very generous to give me such an expensive present.

IV 次の各文の ( ) 内の語を並べかえて意味の通る文にしなさい。
1. He (to / large / has / family / a / support).

2. I (win / am / election / hoping / the / to).

3. She (me / to / the / taught / spell / word / how).

Unit 14　不定詞（2）

A　注意すべき不定詞の用法

1. He *seems* **to be** happy.
   (＝ It seems that he **is** happy.)
2. He *seems* **to have been** happy.
   (＝ It seems that he **was** happy).
3. I was lucky **enough to** find a seat.　「～するほど」
   (＝ I was so lucky that I found a seat.)
4. He is **too** old **to** walk quickly.　「あまり…なので～できない」
   (＝ He is so old that he can't walk quickly.)

B　〈It is ～ for [of] ...to do〉の構文

1. It is necessary *for you* **to start** at once.　「あなたは～することが必要だ」
   [◆ この文は行為についての評価を下す表現であるから、×You are necessary to start at once. と書きかえることはできない]
2. It was careless *of me* **to take** the wrong road.
   「～するなんて私は不注意だった」
   [◆ この文は人についての評価を下す表現であるから、I was careless to take the wrong road. と書きかえることができる]

C　原形不定詞の用法

① 知覚動詞 (**see, hear, feel,** *etc.*)＋目的語＋原形不定詞

1. We *saw* him **cross** the bridge.
2. I *heard* her **come** downstairs.

② 使役動詞 (**make, let, have,** *etc.*)＋目的語＋原形不定詞

3. They *made* us **work** all night.　「（強制的に）～させる」
4. I'll *have* him **shine** your shoes.　「～させる、してもらう」

   【注意】1, 3 の文を受動態にすると、to が必要になる：
   He *was seen* **to cross** the bridge. / We *were made* **to work** all night.

D　原形不定詞を含む慣用表現

1. You'*d better* **eat** more fresh fruit.　「～するほうがよい」
2. I *would rather* **stay** here and **talk** with Dick.　「むしろ～したい」
3. I *cannot but* **admire** his skill.《文語》　「～せずにはいられない」

   【参考】米口語では、3 の代わりに I *cannot help but* **admire** his skill. が用いられることもある。

Fundamental English Grammar

EXERCISE 14

I 次の各文の（ ）内から適切なものを選びなさい。

1. You'd better (eat / to eat) more slowly.
2. It is natural (for / of) you to get angry.
3. The baby was made (drink / to drink) milk.
4. I saw him (enter / to enter) the cafeteria.

II 次の各組の文がほぼ同じ意味になるように、（ ）内に適切な語を入れなさい。

1. It seems that he is a bright student.
   He seems (   ) (   ) a bright student.
2. He is so strong that he can lift the box.
   He is strong (   ) (   ) lift the box.
3. She was so young that she couldn't understand me.
   She is (   ) young (   ) understand me.

III 日本文の意味を表すように、次の各文の（ ）内に適切な語を入れなさい。

1. エレンに皿を洗わせよう。
   I'll (   ) Ellen (   ) the dishes.
2. 私は何かが私の右足に触れるのを感じた。
   I (   ) something (   ) my right foot.

IV 次の各文の意味を書きなさい。

1. It's wrong of you to treat him in that way.

2. I would rather travel by bus than by train.

3. I could not but admit that she was innocent.

V 次の各文の（ ）内の語を並べかえて意味の通る文にしなさい。

1. We (the / often / him / guitar / heard / play).

2. It's (him / you / believe / foolish / to / of).

3. She (to / a / have / cold / seems / had / bad).

不定詞（2）   29

Unit 15　分　詞（１）

　分詞には、「動詞の原形＋ing」の形を持つ**現在分詞**と、「動詞の原形＋ed」または特定の形を持つ**過去分詞**があり、いずれも名詞を修飾する**限定用法**と、補語の働きをする**叙述用法**とがある。

A 分詞の限定用法 ── 分詞が単独で名詞を修飾するときは名詞の前に置かれるが、分詞が他の語句を伴うときは名詞の後に置かれることが多い。一般に、現在分詞は能動的意味を表し、過去分詞は受動的意味を表す。

1. Put the eggs into the **boiling** *water*.　「〜している」
2. This word is not used in **spoken** *English*.
3. Who is the *woman* **sitting** on the bench?　　　　　〈名詞の後〉
4. This is a *motorcycle* **made** in America.

B 分詞の叙述用法

① 主格補語として（主語の状態を述べる）
1. We walked along **singing** folk songs.
2. She sat **surrounded** by her children.
3. He seemed **shocked** by her marriage.

② 目的格補語として（目的語の状態を述べる）
4. He kept me **waiting** for half an hour.
   (I was waiting for half an hour.)
5. The teacher caught a student **cheating**.
   (A student was cheating.)
6. I can't make myself **understood** in Chinese.
   「自分の言葉［考え］を人にわからせる」
   (I am not understood in Chinese.)

③ 知覚動詞＋目的語＋分詞
7. He *heard* his name **called** from behind.
8. I *felt* the floor **shaking**.　「…がゆれているのを」　〈動作の途中〉
   Cf. Did you *feel* the floor **shake**?　「…がゆれるのを」
   　　　　　　　　　　　　　　　　　　　　〈動作の始めから終わりまで〉

④ **have [get]＋目的語＋分詞**
9. I will *have* my socks **washed**.　「〜してもらう」
   Cf. I will *have* her **wash** my socks.　［◆目的語が「人」の場合］
10. He *got* his arm **broken** while he was skiing.　「〜される」　〈被害〉

EXERCISE 15

I 次の各文の ( ) 内の動詞を適切な形に変えなさい。

1. He stood (look) up at the clouds. (　　　　)
2. Who is that girl (dance) with Steve? (　　　　)
3. How beautiful the (rise) sun is! (　　　　)
4. This is a machine (call) a laser printer. (　　　　)
5. There was a (break) cup on the floor. (　　　　)
6. Don't use this word in (speak) language. (　　　　)
7. He is a player (belong) to the baseball team. (　　　　)

II 次の各文の ( ) 内に、下記の語から適切なものを選び、必要に応じて形を変えて入れなさい。

1. He has a lovely daughter (　　　　) Diana.
2. He had his suit (　　　　) by a tailor.
3. That elephant (　　　　) under the tree came from India.
4. I saw a patrol car (　　　　) at full speed.
5. I will have my shoes (　　　　) tomorrow.
6. She lay on the bed (　　　　) to the radio.
7. Have you ever read a poem (　　　　) by Byron?

　　[listen / make / mend / name / pass / stand / write]

III 次の各文の下線部の誤りを正しなさい。

1. I had my watch <u>repair</u> three days ago.

2. He sat on the sofa <u>read</u> the newspaper.

3. I heard a pop song <u>singing</u> in Japanese.

IV 次の各文の ( ) 内の語を並べかえて意味の通る文にしなさい。

1. That (the / in / rated / town / hotel / is / best / as).

2. The girl (brother / with / is / talking / Susie / my).

3. I (him / apples / my / caught / from / stealing / garden).

分　詞 (1)

Unit 16　分　詞（2）

A **分詞構文** ― 分詞に導かれた句が、「時」「理由」「条件」「付帯状況」などの意味で文全体を修飾するものをいう。おもに文語で用いられる。

① 時：when, while, after で書きかえられる。
  1. **Hearing** the sound, I ran out of the room.
     (= *When I heard* the sound, I ran out of the room.)

② 理由：as, because で書きかえられる。
  2. **Not knowing** anyone in town, I felt lonesome.
     (= *As I didn't know* anyone in town, I felt lonesome.)

③ 条件：if で書きかえられる。
  3. **Turning** to the left, you will find the museum.
     (= *If you turn* to the left, you will find the museum.)

④ 譲歩：though または although《文語》で書きかえられる。
  4. **Sitting** in the sun, I still feel cold.
     (= (*Al*)*though I am sitting* in the sun, I still feel cold.)

⑤ 付帯状況：おもに and で書きかえられる。
  5. **Opening** the drawer, she took out his letter.
     (= She opened the drawer, *and took* out his letter.)

     【注意】 分詞の表す「時」が述語動詞の表す「時」より前の場合には、**完了形の分詞構文**（having + 過去分詞）を用いる：**Having locked** all the windows, he went to bed.（ = *After he had locked* all the windows, he went to bed.）

B **独立分詞構文** ― 分詞の意味上の主語と主文の主語が異なる場合は、分詞の前に意味上の主語を置く。

  1. **It being** Sunday, the coffee house was closed.
     (= *As it was* Sunday, the coffee house was closed.)
  2. **The last train having gone**, I had to walk home.
     (= *As the last train had gone*, I had to walk home.)

C **慣用表現となった独立分詞構文**

  1. **Generally speaking**, Americans are outgoing.　「一般的に言って」
  2. **Strictly speaking**, a spider is not an insect.　「厳密に言えば」
  3. **Talking of** baseball, are you a Lions fan?　「…と言えば」
  4. **Judging from** his looks, he is not so young.　「…から判断すると」

EXERCISE 16

I 次の各文を分詞構文を用いて書きかえなさい。

1. Because she felt hot, she took off her overcoat.

2. When I entered his study, I found him sleeping.

3. If you walk faster, you will be in time for school.

4. He left the theater at nine, and arrived home at ten.

II 次の各文を（ ）内の接続詞を用いて書きかえなさい。

1. The snow being deep, the bus was delayed. (as)

2. Having eaten my lunch, I went to the movies. (after)

3. Walking up to me, he said good afternoon. (and)

4. Admitting what he says is possible, I can't agree with him. (though)

5. Turning at the next corner, you will find the hospital. (if)

III 次の各文の意味を書きなさい。

1. Having failed several times, he succeeded at last.

2. Judging from her accent, she must be a Tokyoite.

3. Strictly speaking, history does not repeat itself.

IV 次の各文の（ ）内の語を並べかえて意味の通る文にしなさい。

1. (to / not / what / say / knowing), he remained silent.

2. (the / from / reading / letter / him), she turned pale.

3. (ill / bed / my / being / in / mother), I couldn't go fishing.

分　詞（２）

Unit 17　動名詞（1）

「動詞の原形＋ing」の形で、「～すること」という意味を表す。

A 動名詞の用法 ― 文中で主語・補語・目的語、あるいは前置詞の目的語として用いられる。

1. **Walking** is good for our health. 〈主語〉
2. My hobby is **collecting** model cars. 〈補語〉
3. He really loves **playing** badminton. 〈目的語〉
4. She went away without **saying** a word. 〈前置詞の目的語〉

B 動名詞と不定詞

① 動名詞のみを目的語にとる動詞［群動詞］： avoid, enjoy, finish, mind, give up, put off, *etc.*
1. You must avoid **eating** fatty food.
2. We enjoyed **jogging** in the park.
3. He gave up **smoking** three years ago.

② 不定詞のみを目的語にとる動詞：decide, desire, expect, hope, plan, promise, wish, *etc.*
4. They decided **to sell** the house.
5. I hope **to join** the tennis club.
6. My father promised **to take** us to Nikko.

③ 動名詞と不定詞のどちらも目的語にとる動詞

　(a) 意味が同じもの：attempt, begin, continue, intend, start, *etc.*
7. The prisoners attempted **escaping [to escape]**.
8. He continued **living [to live]** above the store.
9. Where do you intend **going [to go]** this summer?

　(b) 意味が異なるもの：like, forget, hate, remember, try, need, *etc.*
10. a. I like **swimming**.　「～するのが好きだ」　　〈一般的陳述〉
    b. I don't like **to swim** in that river.　「～したい」　〈個別的陳述〉
11. a. I remember **mailing** your letter.　「～した覚えがある」
    b. Remember **to mail** my letter.　「忘れずに～する」
12. a. Sam tried **eating** *natto*, and he liked it.　「ためしに～してみる」
    b. Sam tried **to eat** *natto*, but he couldn't.　「～しようと努める」
13. a. Your hair needs **cutting**.　「～される必要がある」
    b. You need **to cut** your hair.　「～する必要がある」

EXERCISE 17

I 次の各文の（　）内の動詞を適切な形に変えなさい。

1. We enjoyed (skate) on the ice.　　　　　　　（　　　　　）
2. He decided (be) a movie director.　　　　　　（　　　　　）
3. Where do you plan (spend) your vacation?　　（　　　　　）
4. I remember (walk) in the rain with him.　　　（　　　　　）
5. He tried (stand) on his head, but he couldn't.（　　　　　）

II 次の各文の下線部が動名詞であるものを選び、その用法を指摘しなさい。

1. My sister's hobby is <u>making</u> dolls.　　　　　（　　　　　）
2. We stood <u>looking</u> at the children.　　　　　（　　　　　）
3. He makes a living by <u>writing</u> novels.　　　　（　　　　　）
4. She avoided <u>answering</u> my questions.　　　（　　　　　）
5. <u>Looking</u> down, we saw a beautiful lake.　　（　　　　　）

III 次の各組の文を、動名詞と不定詞の用法に注意して和訳しなさい。

1. a. He stopped smoking.
   b. He stopped to smoke.

2. a. I remember shutting the window.
   b. Remember to shut the window.

IV 次の各文の意味を書きなさい。

1. I'll never forget meeting her for the first time.

2. He tried praying, but that didn't ease his mind.

3. I continued living with my parents after getting married.

V 次の各文の（　）内の語を並べかえて意味の通る文にしなさい。

1. I'm (year / to / Kanazawa / hoping / this / visit).

2. He (two / learning / ago / began / years / Spanish).

3. She (going / dark / is / out / afraid / after / of).

Unit 18 　動名詞（2）

A 動名詞の意味上の主語

① 文の主語と一致している場合、一般の人々（we, they など）の場合は、これを明示しない。

1. He is very fond of (×*his*) **playing** cards.
2. (×*Our*) **Singing** together is a lot of fun.

② 文の主語と異なっている場合には、（代）名詞の所有格を動名詞の前に置く。ただし、口語では名詞はそのままの形を用い、代名詞は目的格を用いることが多い。

3. He is proud of *his son*(*'s*) **being** a lawyer. ［◆ his son's は文語］
4. I can't understand *his* [*him*] **leaving** suddenly. ［◆ him は口語］

B 完了形の動名詞（**having** + 過去分詞）— 動名詞の表す「時」が述語動詞の表す「時」よりも以前であることを示したいときに用いる。

1. I regret **having rejected** his offer.
   (= I regret that I *rejected* his offer.)
2. He denied **having opened** the safe.
   (= He denied that he *had opened* the safe.)

C 形容詞として用いられた動名詞 — 動名詞が形容詞として後ろの名詞を修飾することがある（アクセントの位置に注意）。

1. a **dancing** teacher　「ダンス教師」　　　　　　　　　　　〈動名詞〉
   Cf. that **dancing** girl　「あの踊っている女の子」　　　　〈現在分詞〉
2. a **sleeping** car　「寝台車」　　　　　　　　　　　　　　　〈動名詞〉
   Cf. a **sleeping** baby　「眠っている赤ちゃん」　　　　　　〈現在分詞〉
3. a **smoking** room　「喫煙室」　　　　　　　　　　　　　　〈動名詞〉
   Cf. a **smoking** chimney　「煙を出している煙突」　　　　〈現在分詞〉

D 動名詞を含む慣用表現

1. *It is no use* **trying** to talk to him.　「〜してもむだだ」
2. I don't *feel like* **working** today.　「〜したい気がする」
3. I *couldn't help* **feeling** sorry for her.　「〜せずにはいられない」
4. *There is no* **knowing** what will happen.　「〜することができない」
5. You must be careful *in* **crossing** the street.　「〜するときに」
6. *On* **finishing** high school, he went into business.　「〜するとすぐ」

EXERCISE 18

I 次の各文における動名詞の意味上の主語を指摘しなさい。
1. Playing with lighters is dangerous. (　　　　　)
2. I am sure of our team winning the game. (　　　　　)
3. I remember seeing that person somewhere. (　　　　　)
4. He is proud of his mother being a pianist. (　　　　　)

II 次の各組の文がほぼ同じ意味になるように、( ) 内に適切な語を入れなさい。
1. Be careful when you choose your friends.
   Be careful (　　　) (　　　) your friends.
2. As soon as I arrived in Kobe, I telephoned my wife.
   (　　　) (　　　) in Kobe, I telephoned my wife.

III 次の各文を動名詞を用いて書きかえなさい。
1. I am sure he will pass the driving test.

2. There is no hope that he will be saved.

3. Jimmy denied that he had stolen her purse.

IV 次の各文の意味を書きなさい。
1. He regretted having been idle in his youth.

2. There is no going out in this stormy weather.

3. I could not help laughing at his funny story.

V 次の各文の ( ) 内の語を並べかえて意味の通る文にしなさい。
1. I (eating / feel / now / don't / like / anything).

2. It is (advise / no / to / use / her / trying).

3. He is (economics / failed / of / in / having / ashamed).

動名詞（2）

Unit 19　形容詞・副詞

A　形容詞の用法

① 限定用法：名詞の前に置かれて、それを修飾する。ただし、形容詞が他の語句を従えたり、-ingで終わる代名詞を修飾する場合は後置される。

1. She has a **yellow** *ribbon* in her hair.
2. Aomori is a *city* **famous** for its apples.
3. There is *nothing* **new** in his idea.

② 叙述用法：文中で主格補語・目的格補語として用いられる。

4. You look very **tired**.　(You are very tired.)　　　〈主格補語〉
5. The drama made me **sad**.　(I was sad.)　　　〈目的格補語〉

③ 限定用法と叙述用法で意味が異なるもの

6. a. I met *a* **certain** person on the train.　「ある…」
   b. We are **certain** of our victory.　「確信して」
7. a. The **late** Mr. Green was a computer engineer.　「故～」
   b. Mr. White was **late** for work this morning.　「～におくれて」
8. a. The **present** principal is Mrs. Hashimoto.　「現在の」
   b. The principal was **present** at the ceremony.　「～に出席して」

B　副詞の用法 ── 副詞は動詞・形容詞・他の副詞を修飾するが、副詞句・副詞節あるいは文全体を修飾することもある。

1. He *answered* my questions **quickly**.　　　〈動詞を修飾〉
2. George is **very** *good* at painting.　　　〈形容詞を修飾〉
3. She speaks Portuguese **quite** *well*.　　　〈他の副詞を修飾〉
4. The game started **exactly** *at one o'clock*.　　　〈副詞句を修飾〉
5. A man is happy **only** *when he is healthy*.　　　〈副詞節を修飾〉
6. **Clearly** he did not say so.「明らかに」　　　〈文全体を修飾〉

C　注意すべき副詞の用法

1. He tried **hard** to succeed.「懸命に」
2. I could **hardly** hear anything.「ほとんど～しない」
3. The bell has not rung **yet**.「まだ～しない」
4. My grandmother is **still** very strong.「まだ～である」
5. He met her two weeks **ago**.「（今から）…前に」
6. He said that he had met her two weeks **before**.「（その時から）…前に」

EXERCISE 19

I (　) 内の語を適切な位置に補って、次の各文を完成しなさい。

1. He found the bottle of whiskey. (full)

2. My wish is to become a diplomat. (only)

3. I saw something in the distance. (white)

4. This chair is to sit on. (comfortable)

5. Jackson is sometimes for school. (late)

II 次の各文の (　) 内に、下記の語群から適切なものを選んで入れなさい。

1. His advice was (　　　) helpful.
2. Peter is (　　　) losing his car key.
3. (　　　), she knows nothing about it.
4. The game started (　　　) at three o'clock.
5. The old man could (　　　) hear anything.
6. Mr. Kimura came (　　　) into the classroom.

　　　[always / exactly / hardly / slowly / strangely / very]

III 次の各文の意味を書きなさい。

1. He said that he had come here an hour before.

2. Happily, his neck injuries were not serious.

3. Anne moved away, and I don't know her present address.

IV 次の各文の (　) 内の語を並べて意味の通る文にしなさい。

1. We (all / been / hard / day / working / have).

2. He (the / late / is / meetings / for / sometimes / Friday).

3. It (up / still / when / was / woke / dark / she).

Unit 20　比　較（1）

A 基本的な比較表現

① 原級を用いるもの

1. She is *as* **old** *as* Nancy.
2. She is not *as* [*so*] **old** *as* Alice.　「…ほど〜でない」

   【研究】2は「彼女はアリスとおない年ではない」と「彼女はアリスほど年をとっていない（彼女はアリスより若い）」という2通りの意味に用いられるが、前者の意味では as に、後者の意味では old に強勢が置かれる。

② 比較級を用いるもの

3. This suitcase is **heavier** *than* that one.　「…より〜」
4. A horse is **more beautiful** *than* a donkey.

   【参考】比較級を強める副詞には much, far, even などがある：
   This is *much* [*far*] **better** than that.（ずっとよい）／
   It is *even* **more difficult** than I expected.（いっそう難しい）

③ **superior, inferior, senior, junior, prefer** を用いるもの：これらの形容詞や動詞も比較の意味をもっている。比較の対象を表すには、than ではなく to を用いる。

5. This product is **superior [inferior]** *to* that one.
6. David **prefers** walking *to* driving.

④ 最上級を用いるもの

7. He is **the tallest** *of* the three.　「…のうちでいちばん〜」
8. Mt. Everest is **the highest** mountain *in* the world.

   【参考】最上級を強める副詞句には by far がある：
   Harry is *by far* **the best** baseball player.（ずば抜けてうまい野球選手）

B 比較構文の転換 ― 同じ内容を原級・比較級・最上級を用いて表現することができる。

1. a. John cannot run *as* [*so*] **fast** *as* Andy.
   b. Andy can run **faster** *than* John.
2. a. The giraffe is **taller** *than* any other animal.
   b. The giraffe is **the tallest** *of* all animals.
3. a. Nothing is *as* [*so*] **important** *as* love.
   b. Nothing is **more important** *than* love.
   c. Love is **the most important** thing (of all).

EXERCISE 20

I 次の各文の（ ）内に適切な語を入れなさい。
1. Wendy is (　　) sociable than Deborah.
2. He prefers jazz (　　) rock music.
3. Your salary is (　　) higher than mine.
4. She is by (　　) the best ballet dancer.

II 次の各文の（ ）内の語を、必要に応じて適切な形に変えなさい。
1. She is (old) than she looks.　　　　　(　　　　)
2. He swims (well) than the other boys.　(　　　　)
3. The Volga is (long) river in Europe.　(　　　　)
4. My brother drives (carefully) than me.(　　　　)

III 次の各組の文がほぼ同じ意味になるように、（ ）内に適切な語を入れなさい。
1. Iron is more useful than gold.
   Gold is not (　　) useful (　　) iron.
2. This car is superior in design to mine.
   This car is (　　) in design (　　) mine.
3. This room is the same size as that one.
   This room is as (　　) (　　) that one.

IV 次の各文の意味を書きなさい。
1. Soccer is the most popular sport in the world.

2. The area of England is smaller than that of Japan.

3. I have never seen a more beautiful sight than this.

V 次の各文の（ ）内の語を並べて意味の通る文にしなさい。
1. She is (her / more / than / even / sister / cheerful).

2. Nothing is (a / pleasant / sailing / more / yacht / than).

3. This machine (to / one / is / that / quality / superior / in).

比較（1）

Unit 21　比　較（2）

A 注意すべき原級の用法

1. Your house is **twice as** large **as** mine.　「…の2倍〜」
2. You must speak **as** clearly **as** you can.　「できるだけ…」
   (= You must speak **as** clearly **as possible**.)
3. She is **as** pretty **as anyone** in the village.　「だれにも劣らず…」
4. He is **not so much** a composer **as** a conductor.「AというよりはむしろB」
   (= He is a conductor **rather than** a composer.)

B 注意すべき比較級の用法

1. This book is **the thicker of the two**.　「2者のうちでより〜なほう」
2. He is **less** active **than** his brother.　「…ほど〜でない」
   (= He is **not as [so]** active **as** his brother.)
3. She is **more** friendly **than** affectionate.　「BというよりはむしろA」
   〈同一人の異なる性質の比較〉
   Cf. She is friendlier **than** the other girls.　〈別人の同じ性質の比較〉
4. It is getting **warmer and warmer**.　「だんだん…」
5. **The higher** we go up, **the colder** the air becomes.
   「〜すればするほど、ますます…」
   (= As we go up higher, the air becomes colder.)
6. I like him **all the better** *for his faults*.　「それだけいっそう…」
7. A whale is **no more** a fish **than** a horse is.
   (= A whale is **not** a fish **any more than** a horse is.)
   「AがBでないのは、CがBでないのと同じ」

C 注意すべき最上級の用法

1. Even **the wisest** man sometimes makes mistakes.　「どんなに〜でも」
2. She is *a* **most** attractive woman. (most = very)
3. This lake is **deepest** near the island.　〈同一物に関する比較〉
   Cf. This lake is **the deepest** of the five.　〈他との比較〉
4. **Most** children like video games.　「たいていの」
5. You must read **at least** one book a month.　「少なくとも」
6. I can pay only 50 dollars **at (the) most**.　「せいぜい」
7. The cherry blossoms are **at their best** this week.　「見ごろで」

EXERCISE 21

I 次の各文の（ ）内に適切な語を入れなさい。

1. She is a (　　) talkative woman.
2. You must speak as clearly as (　　).
3. Peter is (　　) lucky than clever.
4. This rope is (　　) stronger of the two.

II 次の各組の文がほぼ同じ意味になるように、（ ）内に適切な語を入れなさい。

1. Laura is not as healthy as Sally.
   Laura is (　　) healthy (　　) Sally.
2. She is a dancer rather than a singer.
   She is not (　　) (　　) a singer (　　) a dancer.

III 日本文の意味を表すように、次の各文の（ ）内に適切な語を入れなさい。

1. 彼はその町のだれにも劣らずお金持ちだ。
   He is (　　) rich as (　　) in the town.
2. 2人の少年のうちでアルバートのほうが背が高い。
   Albert is (　　) (　　) of the two boys.
3. 人は年をとればとるほど、ますます口数が少なくなる。
   The (　　) we grow, (　　) (　　) silent we become.

IV 次の各文の意味を書きなさい。

1. I felt all the better for taking a hot bath.

2. A bat is no more a bird than a dog is.

3. The story became more and more exciting.

V 次の各文の（ ）内の語を並べて意味の通る文にしなさい。

1. She (old / 30 / most / is / the / at / years).

2. He (cards / has / least / baseball / at / 100).

3. Most (believe / guilty / he / that / people / is).

比較（2）　43

Unit 22　前置詞

A　基本的な前置詞

1. We stayed **at** an old inn.　　〈場所の一点〉
2. The concert ended **at** nine o'clock.　　〈時の一点〉
3. The party was given **on** Saturday.　　〈曜日〉
4. He will get well **in** a few days.　「…のあとに」　〈時間の経過〉
5. The car stopped **by** the theater.　　〈近接〉
6. He went to Matsuyama **by** plane.　　〈手段〉
7. Cloth is sold **by** the meter.　「1メートルいくらで」　〈単位〉
8. We'll leave **for** Holland next week.　　〈方向〉
9. I bought this radio **for** 30 dollars.　　〈交換〉
10. The town is not far **from** here.　　〈起点〉
11. Mr. Johnson is **from** New York.　　〈出身〉
12. Wine is made **from** grapes.　「…から作られている」　〈原料〉
13. His jacket is made **of** leather.　「…で作られている」　〈材料〉
14. My father died **of** cancer last year.　「…で、のため」　〈原因〉
15. I cut the bread **with** this knife.　　〈道具〉

B　注意すべき前置詞

1. a. We have lived here **for** 15 years.　「…の間」　〈持続期間〉
   b. We live here **during** the summer.　「…の間は」　〈特定の期間中〉
2. a. Wait at my office **till** nine o'clock.　「…まで」　〈継続〉
   b. Come to my office **by** nine o'clock.　「…までに」　〈期限〉
3. a. There is a world map **on** the wall.　　〈接触〉
   b. A lamp was hanging **over** the table.　「…の上に」　〈真上〉
   c. Raise your arm **above** your head.　　〈上方〉
4. a. A ship is passing **under** the bridge.　　〈真下〉
   b. The sun is sinking **below** the horizon.　　〈下方〉

C　群動詞 ─ 2つ以上の語が集まって1つの前置詞と同じ働きをするもの。

1. I stayed at home **because of** the storm.　「～のために」
2. Her failure is **due to** her carelessness.　「～のためで」
3. The water may be carried **by means of** a pipe.　「～によって」
4. **According to** Becky, he's really a good doctor.　「～によれば」
5. They started **in spite of** the heavy rain.　「～にもかかわらず」

EXERCISE 22

I 次の各文の（ ）内から適切なものを選びなさい。
1. Wine is made (by / from / for) grapes.
2. I sold my car (by / for / with) 800 dollars.
3. He hung a picture (at / by / on) the wall.
4. There is a window (above / in / on) the sink.
5. Pencils are sold (at / by / for) the dozen.
6. My father was born (during / on / till) the war.
7. The snow lasted (during / for / since) two days.

II 次の各文（ ）内に適切な前置詞を入れなさい。
1. We have no school (　　) Saturdays.
2. These bags are made (　　) nylon.
3. Scotland is famous (　　) its whisky.
4. I'll finish the work (　　) a few days.
5. Boston is about six miles (　　) here.
6. Come to my new house (　　) your wife.
7. My grandfather died (　　) a heart attack.

III 次の各文の下線部の誤りを正しなさい。
1. They started to Holland last week.

2. The cat was asleep below a chair.

3. A jet plane was flying on the ocean.

4. He did not come back from seven o'clock.

IV 次の各文の（ ）内の語を並べて意味の通る文にしなさい。
1. His success (his / due / work / is / to / hard).

2. The bus (of / was / fog / late / the / because).

3. The load (lifted / crane / of / was / by / a / means).

Unit 23　関係詞（1）

A 関係代名詞 — 代名詞と接続詞の2つの働きをする語で、おもに形容詞節を導く。関係代名詞節が修飾する名詞または代名詞を先行詞という。

1. That is *the man*.　　He asked me the way.　　　　　〈主格〉
   └──────who asked me the way
2. Where is *the notebook*?　　　　I put it on the desk.
   └──────which I put on the desk　　　　　　〈目的格〉

B 関係代名詞の用法

① **who**：先行詞が「人」の場合に用いられる。
  1. The *girl* **who** lives next door is my niece.
  2. I know *a boy* **whose** father is an opera singer.
  3. He has *a lot of friends* **(whom)** he can trust.
     【参考】3のように目的格の関係代名詞は省略されることが多い。

② **which**：先行詞が「物」（動物を含む）の場合に用いられる。
  4. This is *the street* **which** leads to the library.
  5. Have you found *the umbrella* **(which)** you lost?
     【参考】which の所有格は whose または of which であるが、of which は堅苦しい表現なので、口語ではあまり用いられない：
     Look at *the house* **whose** window [the window **of which**] is broken.

③ **that**：先行詞が「人」「物」のいずれの場合にも用いられるが、形容詞の最上級や、all, every, the only, the same, the first, the last, the very などの修飾語句を伴う場合は、とくに that が好んで用いられる。
  6. This is *the highest tower* **(that)** I have ever seen.
  7. Man is *the only animal* **that** can use fire.
  8. This is *the first book* **that** I read in English.
  9. She is *the first nurse* **that** came here yesterday.
  10. You are *the very person* **(that)** I wanted to see.　「まさにその」

C 関係代名詞と前置詞 — 関係代名詞が前置詞の目的語になる場合、前置詞は関係代名詞の前か、関係代名詞の導く節の終わりに置く。

1. That is *the company* **for which** he works.《文語》
2. That is *the company* **(which)** he works **for**.《口語》
   【注意】関係代名詞が that の場合は、必ず前置詞を節の終わりに置く：
   That is *the company* **(that)** he works **for**.

EXERCISE 23

I 次の各文の（ ）内に適切な関係代名詞を入れなさい。

1. Do you know the girl (　　　) has just come in?
2. He is the only person (　　　) can help me.
3. The concert (　　　) she gave ended with fireworks.
4. Use a word (　　　) meaning is clear to you.
5. This is the same car (　　　) was stolen last month.

II 次の2つの文を関係代名詞を用いて1文にしなさい。

1. The man was not at home. I called on him.
2. I have a friend. His sister is studying abroad.
3. This is the magazine. I spoke of it last week.
4. The student is from Indonesia. He sits next to me.
5. The composition was full of mistakes. She wrote it.

III 次の各文の意味を書きなさい。

1. Johnny has a dog which can walk on its hind legs.
2. A wife whose husband is dead is called a widow.
3. Every girl that came to see the show was a teenager.
4. The boy from whom I borrowed the book was my classmate.

IV 次の各文の（ ）内の語を並べて意味の通る文にしなさい。

1. This is (same / I / the / that / lost / watch).
2. He is (all / whom / the / respect / we / professor).
3. The music (very / I / to / that / good / listened / was).

関係詞（1）

Unit 24　関係詞（2）

A **what の用法** ── 先行詞を含む関係代名詞で、「～するもの［こと］」という意味を表す。

1. **What** I like best is reading.
2. He is not **what** he was ten years ago. 「10年前の彼」
3. Show me **what** you have in your left hand.

B **what を含む慣用表現**

1. He is **what we call [what is called]** a bookworm. 「いわゆる」
2. Prof. Suzuki has made me **what I am today**. 「今日の私」
3. He is rich, and **what is better**, very intelligent. 「さらによいことには」
   ☞ その他：what is worse「さらに悪いことには」、what is more「その上」

C **関係副詞の用法** ── 副詞と接続詞の2つの働きをかねる語で、where, when, why, how の4つがある。where は先行詞が「場所」を表す語の場合、when は「時」を表す語の場合、why は「理由」を表す語の場合に用いる。how は常に先行詞なしで用いられる。

1. Nagoya is *the city* **where** she was brought up.
2. Wednesday is (*the day*) **when** I can relax.
3. That's (*the reason*) **why** he changed his job.
4. This is **how** they caught the thief. ［◆ *the way* **how** は誤り］
   【参考】2, 3 のように、関係副詞の先行詞は省略されることがある。

D **限定用法と継続用法** ── 関係詞の導く節が先行詞の意味を限定するものを**限定用法**といい、先行詞の内容を補足的に説明するものを**継続用法**という。継続用法では、ふつう関係詞の前にコンマが置かれる。

1. a. He has *two sons* **who** became dentists. 〈限定用法〉
      ［◆この2人以外に息子がいるかもしれない］
   b. He has *two sons,* **who** (= and they) became dentists. 〈継続用法〉
      ［◆息子はこの2人しかいない］
2. a. I ran to *the place* **where** the accident occurred.
   b. I went to *Osaka,* **where** (= and there) I did some shopping.
3. a. She was born in *the year* **when** the war ended.
   b. He left home *at seven,* **when** (= and then) it began to rain.

EXERCISE 24

I 次の各文の（ ）内に適切な関係詞を入れなさい。

1. I don't believe (　　　　) cannot be seen.
2. Is that the restaurant (　　　　) we will eat?
3. This is (　　　　) he killed the big bear.
4. Tell me the reason (　　　　) you were absent.
5. It was a time (　　　　) there were no cellphones.

II 日本文の意味を表すように、次の各文の（ ）内に適切な語を入れなさい。

1. さらに悪いことには、彼は一人息子を亡くした。
   (　　　　) (　　　　) (　　　　), he lost his only son.
2. そういうわけで、私は「赤毛」というあだ名がついたのです。
   (　　　　) (　　　　) (　　　　) I was nicknamed "Red-head."

III 次の各文を、関係詞の用法に注意して和訳しなさい。

1. a. This is the music box which my aunt gave me.

   b. He gave me an album, which I don't like very much.

2. a. Summer is the season when we can enjoy swimming.

   b. Wait till Thursday, when I will tell you everything.

IV 次の各文の意味を書きなさい。

1. The time will come soon when we can travel to the moon.

2. I want to live in a house where privacy is not disturbed.

3. The book is useful and, what is more, not expensive.

V 次の各文の（ ）内の語を並べて意味の通る文にしなさい。

1. What (is / you / a / sleep / need / good).

2. He (call / is / we / dreamer / what / a).

3. This (how / earned / yen / he / one / is / million).

Unit 25　仮定法（1）

A　仮定法過去

① 現在の事実に反する仮定を表す。「もし（今）～なら、…だろうに」

> If + S { 過去形 / were [was ＜口語＞] } ～、S + { would, should / could, might } + 原形…

1. If I **were [was]** not busy today, I **would go** with you.
   (= Because I am busy today, I will not go with you.)
2. If I **had** enough money, I **could buy** this coat.
   (= As I don't have enough money, I can't buy this coat.)

② 現在または未来に関する単なる仮定を表す。

3. If you **started** now, you **would be** in time.
4. If you **did** as I tell you, you **would succeed**.
   【参考】これに対し、事実を述べた一般的な表現法を**直説法**という。

B　仮定法過去完了 — 過去の事実に反する仮定を表す。「もし（あの時）～していたら、…しただろうに」

> If + S + had + 過去分詞～、S + { would, should / could, might } + have + 過去分詞…

1. If it **had been** fine yesterday, we **would have gone** on a picnic.
   (= As it wasn't fine yesterday, we didn't go on a picnic.)
2. If I **had slept** well last night, I **would** not **be** sleepy now.
   (= I am sleepy now because I didn't sleep well last night.)

C　should と were to による仮定表現：未来の起こりそうもない出来事に対する仮定を表す。「万一～したら」「かりに～するとしたら」などと訳すことが多い。

> If + S { should / were to } + 原形～、S + { would, should / could, might } + 原形…

1. If he **should hear** the news, he **would [will] be** surprised.
2. If he **were to propose** to you, what **would** you **do**?
   【参考】should を用いた仮定では、主節に直説法や命令文がくることもある：
   If he **should come**, tell him I'll be back at five.

EXERCISE 25

I 次の各文の（ ）内の動詞を、必要に応じて適切な形に変えなさい。

1. If he (be) an honest man, I would lend it to him.　（　　　）
2. What will you do if another war (break) out?　（　　　）
3. If she (marry) him, she would be happy now.　（　　　）
4. If I (drink) that water, I would have got sick.　（　　　）
5. If I (have) more time, I would visit the museum.　（　　　）

II 次の各文を仮定法を用いて書きかえなさい。

1. Because I don't know the answer, I can't tell you.

2. As I was not there, I could not save my son's life.

3. He didn't take my advice, so he isn't a rich man now.

III 日本文の意味を表すように、次の各文の（ ）内に適切な語を入れなさい。

1. 万一失敗したら、もう一度やってみるつもりだ。
   If I (　　　) fail, I (　　　) try again.
2. もし私に十分なお金があったら、この望遠鏡が買えるのに。
   If I (　　　) enough money, I (　　　) buy this telescope.

IV 次の各文の意味を書きなさい。

1. If the car had stopped quickly, he would be alive now.

2. If this computer should fail, call the repair department and wait.

3. If I were to go to another planet, I would go to Mars.

V 次の各文の（ ）内の語を並べかえて意味の通る文にしなさい。

1. (of / should / she / success / hear / your / if), she would be glad.

2. (had / if / a / I / worn / raincoat), I would not have got wet.

3. (a / if / were / friend / he / true), he would not deceive you.

Unit 26 仮定法（2）

A　ifの省略 — 文語では、主語と述語動詞の位置を逆にして、ifを省略することがある。

1. **Were it** a little warmer, we *could swim* in the sea.
   (= If it were a little warmer, we could swim in the sea.)
2. **Had I been** in your place, I *would have laughed*.
   (= If I had been in your place, I would have laughed.)

B　if 節のない仮定表現

1. **A man of sense** *would* not *do* such a thing.「分別のある人なら…」
   (= If he were a man of sense, he would not do such a thing.)
2. **But for [Without]** their rescue, I *would have drowned*.「…がなかったら」
   [◆ but for は、文語以外ではあまり用いられない]
   (= If it had not been for their rescue, I would have drowned.)

C　仮定法を含む慣用表現

① **I wish＋主語＋仮定法過去**　「～であればなあ」
   1. **I wish** I *were* as handsome as you.
      (= I am sorry I am not as handsome as you.)

② **I wish＋主語＋仮定法過去完了**　「～していたらなあ」
   2. **I wish** I *had brought* a flashlight.
      (= I am sorry I didn't bring a flashlight.)

③ **It is (high) time＋主語＋仮定法過去**　「もう～してもよいころだ」
   3. **It's (high) time** you *went* to bed.

④ **as if＋主語＋仮定法過去**　「まるで～であるかのように」
   4. He treats me **as if** I *were* only a child.

⑤ **as if＋主語＋仮定法過去完了**　「まるで～したかのように」
   5. She looked **as if** she *had seen* a ghost.

⑥ **if only ~**　「～でありさえすればなあ」
   6. **If only** I *were* ten years younger!
      (= I wish I were ten years younger.)

⑦ **if it were not for ~**　「もし～がなければ」
   7. **If it were not for** music, the world *would be* a dull place.

⑧ **if it had not been for ~**　「もし～がなかったら」
   8. If it **had not been for** the storm, we *would have arrived* earlier.

EXERCISE 26

I 次の各文の（　）内の動詞を、必要に応じて適切な語に変えなさい。

1. I wish I (know) Anna's telephone number.　（　　　　）
2. It's high time you (have) a haircut.　（　　　　）
3. He looked as if he (just get) out of bed.　（　　　　）
4. (Be) I a teacher, I would give easier tests.　（　　　　）

II 次の各組の文がほぼ同じ意味になるように、（　）内に適切な語を入れなさい。

1. She talks just like a young girl.
   She talks (　　　) (　　　) she (　　　) a young girl.
2. But for water, we could not live.
   If it (　　　) (　　　) (　　　) water, we could not live.

III 次の各文を（　）内の指示に従って書きかえなさい。

1. I am sorry he was not at home then.（if only を用いて）

2. We ought to discuss the matter.（it's time... を用いて）

3. I am sorry I am not as healthy as you.（I wish... を用いて）

IV 次の各文の意味を書きなさい。

1. This medicine might cure your headache.

2. Without your help, I would not have succeeded.

3. I wish I had not said such rude things to him.

V 次の各文の（　）内の語を並べかえて意味の通る文にしなさい。

1. I wish (had / then / with / she / been / me).

2. But for his idleness, (good / he / be / man / would / a).

3. Should you miss the train, (noon / there / not / you / before / get / would).

Short Readings

Unit 1　名　詞

次の各文を日本語に訳しなさい。

(1)　There was a roar as the burners fired up. We rocked a little in our basket, and then we went higher and higher. The sky was turning from grey to pastel pink. The sun would soon rise over the horizon. We were taken quietly over fields and banana trees. When we passed over a village, the children came running out. We threw out bags of candies to them. The great temple could be seen near a patch of jungle. I was thrilled with the experience. I was fulfilling a dream I had had for many years; to fly over Angkor Wat in a hot air balloon.

【Notes】 **roar**「爆音」、**fire up**「～を始動させる」、**rock**「揺れ動く」、**basket**「(気球の) 吊りかご」、**take over~**「～を運んで行く」、**pass over~**「～を横切る」、**come out**「出て来る」、**throw out~**「～を投げ出す」、**a patch of~**「～の一区画」、**be thrilled with~**「～にわくわくしている」、**fulfill~**「～をかなえる」

(2)　I'd like to invite you all to my apartment. Unfortunately, you can't all come at once. It's a very small apartment, but I like it. Everything is at my fingertips. When I sit at the dining table, all I have to do is stretch my arm to the left, open the fridge, and take out whatever I want for lunch. If I want a warm meal, I turn to the right, put some ingredients into the pressure cooker, and cook a vegetable soup or a meat stew. When I sit in the reclining chair, I just lean my head back and look up at the white ceiling. Instead of a television, a projector lights up and I watch the news.

【Notes】 **you all**「みなさん全員」、**apartment**「アパートの部屋」、**at one's fingertips**「手もとにある」、**all I have to do**「私がすべき全てのこと」、**fridge**「冷蔵庫」、**take out~**「～を取り出す」、**ingredient**「食材」、**pressure cooker**「圧力鍋」、**lean ~ back**「～を後ろに傾ける」、**light up**「点灯する」

(3)　"You might say that tomatoes are red, and strawberries, too. But is it really the same red?" asks Takeshi. He is not the comedian, Beat Takeshi, nor the movie director, Takeshi Kitano, but Takeshi, the painter. Art Takeshi is an art show which displays the work of the painter, Takeshi Kitano. Born in Tokyo in 1947, Takeshi has experienced much over the years. He, himself, says that he likes cars, money, and cats, and those three things seem to be recurring themes in his paintings. Takeshi's art also includes humor. He admires the paintings done by children. "Children are geniuses," he says.

【Notes】 **movie director**「映画監督」、**art show**「展覧会」、**work**「作品」、**over the years**「長年にわたり」、**recurring themes**「繰り返し扱われるテーマ」、**admire~**「～を賞賛する」

56　Fundamental English Grammar

Unit 2　冠　詞

次の各文を日本語に訳しなさい。

(1) "Look at that!" exclaimed John. Mariko asked what he wanted her to look at. "Look at the roof of that old building! It has stones on it!" said John, showing surprise. Mariko then told him that, long ago, roofs were made of wooden planks and stones were placed on top of them to stop the planks from blowing away in a storm. She said that the design of a building depended on the climate of the area. "In some areas, you will see steep thatched roofs. A lot of snow falls there. But here, on Sado Island, we get a lot of storms. We need something to stop the roof from blowing away," she explained.

【Notes】plank「厚板」、stop A from doing「Aが〜するのを防ぐ」、blow away「（風）に飛ばされる」、depend on〜「〜よって決まる」、steep thatched roofs「急勾配のかやぶき屋根」

(2) Once a year in October or November, many writers from all over Japan gather for a two-day conference. It is very popular. Even some writers from overseas come. Of course, there are presentations on, for example, how someone wrote a travel book, or how someone else translated a book of poetry. Children's book illustrators also come to show some of their drawings. There are many workshops, too. The workshops help writers get new ideas. Editors, too, come to the conference. They are always looking for new talent. Young writers hope to be discovered by an editor from a big-name company.

【Notes】two-day「2日間の」、on〜「〜について」、travel book「旅行記」、children's book illustrators「子ども絵本の作家」、drawing「デッサン」、workshop「研修講座」、help A do「Aが〜するのに役立つ」、editor「編集者」、talent「才能のある人」、big-name「有名な」

(3) A pack of a dozen eggs cannot be called heavy, but when the pack becomes trays of thirty stacked to ten or twenty tiers high, the load will become very heavy and it will become difficult to keep one's balance. The whole load may easily spill over onto the floor. That's when robots can help. The word *robota* is Slavic, and means "labor". Indeed, many factories are now run almost entirely by robots. The robot is like a carpenter, or a painter, or a construction worker. Robots can carry parts and screw in screws, and do other things that are too difficult for people to do.

【Notes】tray of thirty「一皿に30（の卵）」、stack〜「〜を積み重ねる」、tier「層」、load「積荷」、keep one's balance「バランスを保つ」、spill over「こぼれる、ずれ落ちる」、when〜「〜する時」、Slavic「スラブ語」、run〜「〜を運営する」、screw in screws「ねじを止める、ねじで取り付ける」

Short Readings

Unit 3　代名詞（1）

次の各文を日本語に訳しなさい。

(1) How often do you check the weather forecast? Some people like to check it several times a day: in the morning newspaper, on the evening T.V. news, as well as on their computers at work. Do you think that the weather forecast is reliable? Japanese weather forecasts are considered to be very accurate, but not everybody believes their weather forecasters. Londoners, in particular, say they prefer to take a collapsible umbrella and a light jacket with them every day, as it may start as a sunny day, change to rain or wind by lunch, and become quite cold in the evening.

【Notes】 weather forecast「天気予報」、 A as well as B「Bと同様にAも」、 at work「仕事中の」、 reliable「信頼できる」、 not everybody~「すべての人が~ではない」、 weather forecaster「天気予報士」、 Londoner「ロンドン子」、 take~「~を携帯する」、 collapsible umbrella「折りたたみ傘」

(2) Do you find learning a foreign language difficult? Many people do. But some enjoy it. Tim Doner is a polyglot. He is a young American who has taught himself to speak over twenty languages. When he was 13, he became interested in Hebrew and then Arabic. Then he tried Russian, Italian, Persian, Swahili, Chinese and many more. He learns from grammar books, flash cards, and songs. Tim says he doesn't aim to become perfect. He says he loves history and uses the languages to learn the history and culture of various countries from the people who know it best.

【Notes】 find A B「AをBと感じる」、 some~「~の人もいる」、 polyglot「数カ国語を使いこなす人」、 teach oneself「独学する」、 many more「さらに多くの（言語）」、 aim to do「~しようと目指す」

(3) We often see flamingoes when we go to a zoo or aviary. Flamingoes are like stars. Many cameras point in their direction. It is their pretty pink color that makes them so popular with children and adults alike. In fact, their name comes from Spanish, and means "flame-colored." But the flamingo itself is not a pink bird. Flamingoes are pink because of the food they eat. Flamingoes eat tiny shrimp and algae. The more algae they eat, the deeper the color of their wings. Flamingoes are originally from Africa, South-west Asia, and Southern America.

【Notes】 aviary「飼鳥園」、 point「向く」、 in one's direction「~の方向に」、 It is ~ that は強調構文、 come form~「~に由来する」、 flame-colored「燃えるような色」、 algae「藻」、 The＋比較級~, the＋比較級 ...「~すればするほど…」

Unit 4　代名詞（2）

次の各文を日本語に訳しなさい。

(1)　"She comes here by herself every evening," said the priest to the police officer. "Both of her children are dead. One died in a car accident two years ago, and the other in a plane crash last year," added the priest. The police officer listened carefully, and nodded. He asked what time she came, and how long she spent there praying. He asked specifically about the night of the murder. Although he did not think that the woman was the one he was looking for, he had to ask questions. Murder in a small town was not an everyday event. He hoped to solve the matter soon.

【Notes】 **priest**「牧師」、**police officer**「警察官」、**specifically**「とりわけ」、**murder**「殺人事件」、**everyday event**「日常よくあること」

(2)　Judy was in the mood for pancakes. She searched the cupboard for the ingredients. "Do we have any flour?" she called to her mother, but she didn't wait for an answer. "Got it!" she called. She took down the vanilla essence and baking powder, as well. Then she went to the fridge. There she found neither eggs nor milk. "We don't have any milk or eggs. Will somebody buy me some milk and some eggs," she said, facing her father who was sleeping on the couch. Mother left father sleeping, and quickly went to buy the ingredients for the pancakes.

【Notes】 **in the mood for~**「～をしたい（食べたい）気分」、**search A for B**「BがないかとAを探す」、**ingredient**「材料」、**flour**「小麦粉」、**get it**「見つけた」、**take down~**「～を降ろす、取り出す」、**baking powder**「ふくらし粉」、**facing~**「～の方を向きながら」（分詞構文・付帯状況）、**couch**「ソファー」、**leave A B**「AをBの状態にしておく」

(3)　The train stood waiting at platform 7. It was a small local train with only two carriages. Susan walked up to the first door. It didn't open. She went to another. Again, the door didn't open. Susan noticed a small bright button to the left of the door. She wondered what it was for. Still, the door did not open. She stood at each door on each carriage. At last, the final door opened. Someone stepped out and Susan got in. As the train started to move, Susan heard an announcement: "The doors do not open automatically. Please press the green button, and open the door yourself."

【Notes】 **stand**「停車している」、**local train**「各駅停車の列車」、**carriage**「客車」、**walk up to~**「～に近寄る」、**bright**「光っている」、**wonder~**「～かと思う」、**what~for**「～は何の目的か」、**still**「依然として」、**step out**「表に出る」

Unit 5　時　制

次の各文を日本語に訳しなさい。

(1)　　Gifu City lies on the banks of the Nagara River, almost exactly in the center of Honshu. The city is famous for its 1300-year-old tradition of cormorant fishing, and its connection with Oda Nobunaga, who gave the city its name. The word "Gifu" is said to be a combination of two Chinese place names: 「岐」from Qishan, a mountain in China where unification of the country occurred, and 「阜」from Qufu, the town where Confucius was born. Gifu Castle stands at the top of Mt. Kinka. From there you can look down over the river and the city.

【Notes】**lie**「位置する」、**bank**「川岸」、**cormorant fishing**「鵜飼い（鵜を使った漁）」、**connection with~**「～との関係」、**Qishan**「岐山、チーシャン」、**unification**「統一」、**Qufu**「曲阜、チューフー」、**Confucius**「孔子」、**Mt. Kinka**「金華山」、**look down**「見下ろす」、**over~**「～一面を」

(2)　　The wind blew in my face. It was a warm wind. I saw seagulls bobbing up and down on the water. Others flew overhead. Some came close to the dock. Then the ferry came. It was bigger than I thought it would be. We walked up the narrow plank. First I went to my cabin. It was small. There was a bunk bed and a tiny desk. A round window gave me a view of the ocean. I felt excited. It was the first time for me to go overseas by ship. We left Osaka at 3 o'clock in the afternoon, and arrived in South Korea at 10 o'clock the next morning. I wanted to see the Inland Sea, but we passed through during the night.

【Notes】**blow**「吹く」、**in one's face**「まともに」、**bob up**「ぱっと浮かび上がる」、**on the water**「海上で」、**dock**「船着き場」、**plank**「渡り板」、**bunk bed**「二段ベッド」、**a view of~**「～の景色」、**South Korea**「韓国」、**the Inland Sea**「瀬戸内海」、**pass through**「通過する」

(3)　　"I want to be in the Olympics," said Ben one day after watching a program about the Olympics on T.V.

　　"But you won't be able to join the next Olympics," said his mother, adding that he was still too young, and didn't even like to play sport.

　　"Ah, yes. You are right," said Ben. "I will tell you how I am going to do it. I shall be an interpreter. I can speak English already. I will study French this year and Spanish next year. I shall help guide the athletes from overseas around the Olympic Village."

【Notes】**the Olympics** = the Olympic games「オリンピック大会」、**adding that~**「～と付け加えて言う」（分詞構文・付帯状況）、**help (to) do**「～して助ける」、**Olympic**（形）「オリンピックの」

Unit 6　進行形

次の各文を日本語に訳しなさい。

(1)　They say that Tuvalu is disappearing. The water is rising and the environment of Tuvalu is changing. Tuvalu is an island nation in the Pacific Ocean. It is the 4th smallest country in the world. Because it is so far from other countries, tourism is not an important industry here. There were only 360 tourists in 2016, but the number is increasing. Now, volunteers are coming to help plant mangroves. During the wet season, between November and April, floods and high tides are always damaging crops. By planting mangroves, they are trying to stop flooding.

【Notes】 **they say that~**「～だと言われている」、**Tuvalu**「ツヴァル」（珊瑚島の国）、**water**「海水面」、**plant~**「～を植える」、**wet season**「雨期」、**flood**「洪水」、**high tide**「高潮」

(2)　I met Marion at the War Memorial. She and her friends had come on a cruise ship. "We are sailing home this evening," she said. I asked if she had any family who had died in the war here. "No, but I'm so glad that I came. My granddaughter is marrying a man from Okinawa next month. Learning about the culture and the music, and the food, too, was a wonderful experience." She smiled, and then she paused. "You see, I was riding my bicycle near the harbor that day. I saw the bombs falling on our ships." The hand holding the walking stick trembled, and then she slowly went away.

【Notes】 **War Memorial**「戦没者記念館」、**cruise ship**「大型観光船」、**pause**「ためらう」、**you see**「よく聞いてね」、**walking stick**「杖」、**go away**「立ち去る」

(3)　Mr. Suda looked at the class. "This month, we shall be studying Shakespeare. In particular, we will be looking at phrases coined by Shakespeare." Some students were looking a little bored. The professor raised his voice. "If you want to become high school teachers, you must study Shakespeare. Do you know about the legacy that Shakespeare left us?" They didn't. He was still mumbling about 'a heart of gold' and the 'the be-all and end-all' of things when the bell rang. "Don't let yourself become a 'laughing stock'," he shouted. "Ah, 'in my heart of hearts' I know you want to learn," he added.

【Notes】 **Shakespeare (1564~1616)**「英国劇作家、詩人」、**look at~**「～を調べる」、**coin~**「～を作り出す」、**raise one's voice**「大きな声で言う」、**mumble**「もぐもぐ言う」、**a heart of gold**「思いやりのある心」、**the be-all and end-all**「最も重要な要素・肝心なこと」（マクベス）、**things**「物事」、**laughing stock**「物笑いの種」、**in one's heart of hearts**「心の奥底で」（ハムレット）

Unit 7　完了形（1）

次の各文を日本語に訳しなさい。

(1)　Have you ever been to the top of a really tall building? Have you been to the viewing platform near the top of Tokyo Skytree, or to the Shanghai World Financial Centre? The Marina Bay Sands Hotel in Singapore isn't as high as some others, but the view is just as spectacular. I have been to the top of the Marina Sands only once, but I would love to go again. At the top, you can swim in the world's highest pool, or look out over a harbor full of ships and yachts. I have never seen such a sunset as the one from the Ce La Vie Restaurant, an open restaurant at the top of the Marina Bay Sands.

【Notes】**viewing platform**「展望台」、**Shanghai World Financial Centre**「上海ワールドフィナンシャルセンター」、**just as spectacular (as some others)**「同じくらい壮大な」、**look out over~**「~全体を見渡す」、**Ce La Vie Restaurant**「セラヴィレストラン」、**open**「広々とした」

(2)　"Sorry for being late," said Ben, red in the face from running. "I've been working on the project since yesterday. I haven't slept at all," he added. But Ben didn't look sleepy. Instead, he looked excited. His hair was messy and his clothes were creased, but his eyes shone. "I think I have just found a way to save us $30,000 a year." His plan was to cut down on office space. He said that less office space would mean less electricity for lighting and air-conditioning. Someone asked what all the office workers would do. "Easy," he said. "Send them home. Let them work on projects from home."

【Notes】**red in the face from running**「走ってきたので顔が赤い」、**work on~**「~に取り組む」、**instead**「それどころか」、**messy**「きたない」、**crease**「しわが寄った」、**save A B**「AにBを節約する」、**cut down on~**「~を切り詰める」、**office worker**「（会）社員」

(3)　When Typhoon Lionrock, the 10th of the season, made landfall in northern Japan, it had already caused blackouts and had brought traffic to a standstill. Residents were told to leave their homes and gather in an evacuation shelter. The Meteorological Agency had sent out a warning to people to stay away from the coastline. More than 100 flights and all bullet train services going to or from the Tohoku region had been cancelled. Just five years after the 2011 tsunami and earthquake, the people of Ofunato and Ishinomaki cities were again battling nature.

【Notes】**landfall**「上陸」、**blackout**「停電」、**bring A to a standstill**「Aを停止する」、**evacuation shelter**「避難所」、**The Meteorological Agency**「気象庁」、**send out~**「~を発表する」、**bullet train**「新幹線」、**service**「運行」、**to or from the Tohoku…** =to the Tohoku or from the Tohoku…

Fundamental English Grammar

Unit 8 完了形（2）

次の各文を日本語に訳しなさい。

(1) I had been sitting by the window all the way in seat 8D. I had especially asked for a window seat because I had wanted to watch the scenery. I had brought my camera as well. After nearly two hours, the train stopped at a busy station. In came a crowd of new passengers. I had just started to eat my lunch when a man looked down at me. "I think you are in the wrong seat. This is my seat!" he said. He was right. My ticket said Car 8, seat 9D. I had to move. But by the time I gathered my things and went to my seat, someone had already taken my window seat. I sighed. It was not a good day.

【Notes】 **all the way**「ずっと」、**window seat**「窓側の席」、**busy**「にぎやかな（交通量の多い）」、**In came a crowd of new passengers.** = A crowd of new passengers came in.　**look down**「見おろす」、**say~**「～と（書いて）ある」、**things**「持ち物」、**not a good day**「ついていない日」

(2) It was the last house in a dead-end street. It had been painted a pretty light blue, but now the walls were dirty and some of the windows were broken. Everyone said the house had been empty for many, many years. Tommy said it was haunted. Then I saw a shadow in the front window. Tommy was sure that the shadow was a ghost. We went to take a closer look. We entered the garden. It seemed that someone had just cut the grass. We were just talking about ghosts when he came to the door. Tommy screamed and ran away. I stayed and became friends with Mr. Joel, aged 93.

【Notes】 **a dead-end street**「袋小路」、**haunted**「幽霊のでる」、**front window**「（家の）正面の窓」、**be sure that~**「～と確信する」、**take a closer look**「よく見る」、**grass**「草」

(3) For some people, life is one adventure after another. When I asked Mr. Rowe and his wife how long they had been teaching, Mr. Rowe replied, "In March, we will have been teaching for nine years. Before that, I was a pilot and my wife was a cabin attendant. We had never thought about teaching before our first holiday here. We liked the country so much that we both got our TEFL diplomas." I asked them if they had ever felt homesick. "Rarely, until the birth of our first grandchild," said Mrs. Rowe. "The dear boy will have already grown up by the time I see him," she said sadly.

【Notes】 **adventure**「意外な経験」、**never ~ before...**「…まで～することはなかった」、**TEFL** = Teaching English as a Foreign Language「外国語としての英語教授法」、**dear**「かわいい」

Unit 9　助動詞（1）

次の各文を日本語に訳しなさい。

 (1)　Travelling can be very inconvenient without a train pass. You must always have enough money in your pocket to buy a ticket, and if it is at peak hour, it can take some time to buy that ticket. You need to check the price, then stand in line. It is all so troublesome. It is so much easier if you have a card. No checking of prices and no waiting in front of ticket vending machines. You can pass through the wicket smoothly. You may need to top up the card occasionally, but it is so much more convenient to travel with a train pass, than to go without one.

【Notes】**train pass**「プリペイド乗車カード」、**peak hour**「（交通量の）ピーク時」、**some time**「かなり長い時間」、**that ticket**「（購入したい）あの切符」、**stand in line**「列に並ぶ」、**so much**「それだけ」、**ticket vending machine**「自動券売機」、**pass through~**「〜を通り抜ける」、**wicket**「改札」、**top up~**「〜をチャージする」、**without one** = without a train pass

 (2)　Eriko knocked on the door. "May I come in?" she said in a shaky voice. "Yes, you may," answered the man sitting at the desk inside the room. Eriko slowly opened the door. Her interview exam had begun. The man waved his hand towards the chair. "Please, sit down. You can put your bag in the brown basket." She did that. "You must be very nervous," the man said. "You look very pale." He smiled, and Eriko began to relax. Gradually, as the interview progressed, Eriko became more confident. By the end of the interview, Eriko had a broad smile on her face.

【Notes】**shaky**「震える」、**interview exam**「面接試験」、**wave one's hand towards~**「〜の方へ手で合図する」、**look pale**「顔色が悪い」、**confident**「自信のある」、**broad**「明らかな」

 (3)　Professor Brown was very popular with his students. He was tall and lean, and he enjoyed outdoor sports. His biggest secret was his age. Many tried to guess it.

"He must be over 50. His hair is grey," said one girl.

"He can't be more than 40," said one boy. "He is so fit, and he looks so young."

"I hear he used to be a sumo wrestler. Can you believe it?" said another.

"One must not believe everything one is told," said the first student, and then added "I hear that he has travelled to over 40 countries." And so talk continued.

【Notes】**lean**「やせた」、**guess~**「〜を言い当てる」、**fit**「元気な」、**one**「人」

64　Fundamental English Grammar

Unit 10　助動詞（2）

次の各文を日本語に訳しなさい。

 (1)　"Perhaps you should talk to the doctor about it," suggested the nurse as Mr. Bridges got up. His blood pressure was a little high and he wasn't feeling as energetic as usual. He knew he ought to sit at the computer less and exercise more, but it was difficult. He remembered the days when he used to walk his dog every evening. But the dog had died of old age. He was alone now, and would spend his time watching T.V. all day. But the doctor was very firm. He advised that Mr. Bridges either take some medicine or exercise more.

【Notes】suggest~「~してはと言う」、energetic「元気な」、as usual「いつものように」、spend A ~ing「~してAを過ごす」、firm「（意思）が堅い」、advise~「~を指示する」

 (2)　Bennelong Point is a place that many people know. However, it is not unusual that you should not know its name. Bennelong Point is the site of the Sydney Opera House. It is said that an Aboriginal man called Bennelong asked if a hut could be built for him there. Originally, the place was a small rocky island. Between 1818 and 1821, the area between the island and the mainland was filled with rocks. Then it was made into a level platform. Before the Sydney Opera House was built there, Bennelong Point was the home of the Tram Depot.

【Notes】Bennelong Point「ベネロング・ポイント」（Bennelongは白人と先住民の仲介者）、site「場所」、Aboriginal「アボリジニ人の」（豪と周辺の先住民族）、hut「小屋」、mainland「本土」、level platform「平地」、home「列車の基地」、Tram Depot「路面電車」

 (3)　Junko was a proud girl. She chose her friends carefully. She wouldn't talk much with people she didn't like. She did well in her studies, and was very competitive. She wasn't very good at sport, but she was an enthusiastic spectator, even when she ought not to have made so much noise. She liked winners and winning. One day, she looked very depressed indeed. "She must have failed the national exam," whispered one friend to another. They were all a little afraid to ask. Then a teacher came up to her and, with a friendly smile, said, "Don't worry. Life is full of ups and downs."

【Notes】proud「高慢な」、do well in one's study「勉強がよくできる」、enthusiastic spectator「熱狂的な観客」、make so much noise「大いに盛り上がり騒ぐ」、national exam「国家試験」、friendly smile「親しみを込めた微笑み」、ups and downs「浮き沈み」

Unit 11　態（1）

次の各文を日本語に訳しなさい。

(1)　The judge laid all thirty-five photographs out on the desks. The photos had been taken by high school students. As a professional photographer, Mark had been asked to judge the school photo contest. Mark looked at the photos, one by one. Some were taken of the nearby field of sunflowers: the contrast of blue sky and yellow flowers was pretty. Some were taken at the local festival: people crowded around floats. Then Mark spotted a photo of a white sandy beach at sunset. "This is excellent," he said to himself. He made a note of the student's name.

[Notes] **judge**「審査員」、**lay out~**「~を陳列する、広げる」、**some** = some photos、**crowd around**「群がる」、**float**「山車（だし）」、**spot~**「~を見つける」、**at sunset**「日没時の」、**make a note of~**「~をメモに取る」

(2)　Do you know what a *tento-mushi* is called in English? It is called a "lady-bird" or "lady-bug." It is called a "bird" because of its wings. It is a "bug" because it is an insect. But why "lady"? Scholars say that the term was first used in France. The ladybird was given this name because it eats other pests like aphids, which are a big problem for the farmer. In other words, ladybirds help the poor farmer, just as Mother Mary, known to Christians as "Our Lady", is said to have helped the poor people centuries ago.

[Notes] **bug**「虫」、**insect**「昆虫」、**term**「用語」、**pest**「害虫」、**aphid**「アブラムシ」、**as~**「~と同様に」、**Our Lady**「聖母マリア」

(3)　The name "Baumkuchen" comes from the rings that look like tree growth rings. The German name means "tree cake." It is made by spreading thin layers of cake mix on a log while rolling it and cooking it. Typically, it is made up of 15 to 20 layers. Sometimes, the outside is covered with icing or chocolate. Although the cake can be found in many countries in Europe, it was first introduced into Japan by a German chef called Karl Juchheim. Now, not only the Juchheim brand, but also many other bakery shops produce this delicious cake.

[Notes] **come from~**「~に由来する」、**tree growth ring**「年輪」、**spread A on B**「AをBの上に広げる」、**layer**「層」、**log**「（生地）棒」、**typically**「一般的に」、**be made up of~**「~でできている」、**cover A with B**「AをBでおおう」、**icing**「砂糖衣」、**Karl Juchheim**「カール・ユーハイム」（独人菓子職人）

Unit 12　態（2）

次の各文を日本語に訳しなさい。

(1)　Today I went in search of a castle that never was. When I imagine a castle, I think of a big, solid building, many storeys high, like Osaka Castle. That is not what I found. Beside the moat which used to surround the castle of Toyama, there is a castle tower. It is fairly new. It was built after World War II, to encourage the people to rebuild their community. From the top, you can see where the original castle stood. But there was never a tall castle like the one in Osaka. Toyama Castle was a spacious single-storey mansion with a lovely garden.

【Notes】 **in search of~**「～を捜して」、**that never was**「見たことなかった」、**solid**「強固な」、**storey**「階層」、**moat**「堀」、**castle tower**「天守閣」、**encourage A to do**「Aに～するよう励ます」、**mansion**「館」

(2)　The topic of English education is being discussed by people all over Japan. If English is taught in primary schools, will the Japanese people be able to speak English more fluently? Many people think so. Some people say that as the style of teaching English changes, the English ability of the teachers will also improve. Up until now, many school textbooks have been written with a focus on teaching conversation. Now, the focus seems to be on reading. The more a person reads, the better that person can write. Newspapers or novels: the wider one reads, the more topics one can talk about too.

【Notes】 **topic**「話題」、**primary school**「小学校」、**fluently**「流ちょうに」、**English ability**「英語能力」、**up until now**「これまで」、**school textbook**「教科書」、**with a focus on~**「～に焦点をあてて」、**the more~, the better…**「～すればするほど、ますます…」

(3)　Shirakawa-go and Gokayama were designated as World Heritage Sites in 1995. The area is known for its thatched roof houses. Visitors are surprised to learn that the upper storeys of the houses were used to raise silkworms while the family lived on the ground floor. One house, the Wada Mansion, is very interesting. It has two entrances. One entrance was for the family and local visitors. The other was for the Buddhist priests and special government officials who came to visit from Takayama. Now the house is open to the public.

【Notes】 **Shirakawa-go and Gokayama**「白川郷・五箇山の合掌造り集落」（岐阜）、**designate~**「～を登録する」、**World Heritage Site**「世界遺産」、**thatched roof**「かやぶき屋根」、**upper storey**「上階」、**raise silkworm**「蚕を飼育する」、**ground floor**「1階」、**the Wada Mansion**「和田家住宅」、**one… the other**「一つは、もう一つは」、**open to the public**「一般に開放されている」

Unit 13　不定詞（1）

次の各文を日本語に訳しなさい。

(1)　"Don't eat or drink anything after 9 p.m." That is what I was told. It was not easy to skip breakfast when everyone around me was enjoying their slice of toast or bowl of cereal. I didn't know what to do to stop myself from going to the coffee maker. I was hungry and thirsty! I sat in front of the T.V. I watched the news: a car accident in Kyushu, a theft in Tokai, a murder in Tohoku. Then, a new menu for a popular airline! Delicious wine. Tasty steak. Creamy-white cheese cake. It all looked so good. My tummy rumbled. At last it was time to go to the hospital for a blood test.

【Notes】**skip~**「～を抜く」、**enjoy~**「～をおいしく食べる」、**cereal**「コーンフレーク」、**stop A from doing**「Aが～するのを止める」、**airline**「航空会社」、**delicious**「香りの良い」、**tasty**「おいしい」、**tummy**「おなか」、**rumbled**「ゴロゴロ鳴る」、**blood test**「血液検査」

(2)　"Where do you think you'll be in five or ten years?" This is a question that is often asked at an interview for a job. The answer is often the final thing that influences the company's decision. Take, for example, a young chef wanting to work in a new restaurant. If he says "In five years, I want to be head chef, and in 10 years, I want to open my own restaurant in my home town," he will probably get the job. It shows that he wants to learn, and that he has a dream. This type of person will certainly try to do his best. If he says "I don't know," he probably won't get the job. He shows no ambition.

【Notes】**interview for a job**「就職面接」、**final**「最終的な」、**take A for example**「Aを例にとる」、**head chef**「料理長」、**show that~**「～ということを証明する」、**learn**「技術を習い覚える」、**certainly**「きっと、確かに」、**do one's best**「がんばる、ベストを尽くす」

(3)　Mr. Nox's office was on the top floor. I took the elevator up. I stepped out of the elevator and into a cold, silent hallway. At first, I didn't know which door to go to. Then I saw it; a dark green door with golden letters. I knocked on the door. A very tall woman opened the door. "Oh, Mr. Hayashi. We are very pleased to see you. Please, come in." I was happy to see that both Mr. Nox and his secretary were smiling. I had heard that Mr. Nox was a hard person to please. Their smiles meant that my business proposal was going to be successful.

【Notes】**top floor**「最上階」、**out of~**「～の外へ」、**see~**「～に気がつく」、**be pleased to do**「～してうれしい」、**business proposal**「事業計画」、**successful**「好結果をおさめた」

Unit 14　不定詞（2）

次の各文を日本語に訳しなさい。

 (1)　Things are not always as they seem. Take Ben's case, for example. Ben seemed to be unhappy in his job. He complained often. "The company makes us work all night! It's terrible!" he said. His friends were surprised. They sympathized with him. But after asking him some questions, his friends learnt that Ben had actually chosen to work at night because the night shift paid more. In every situation, it is necessary for us to get the facts. Rather than having a cruel boss, Ben had been lucky enough to find a job that paid him well.

【Notes】things「物事」、not always「いつも〜とは限らない」、sympathize with〜「〜に同情する」、learn that〜「〜ということを知る」、choose to do「〜することに決める」、night shift「夜勤」、pay「もうかる」、A rather than B「BというよりむしろA」

 (2)　The Chingay Parade is a very popular event. It is held in Singapore, usually at the end of February. It started as a noisy event to welcome the Chinese New Year. May Lee, a Chinese Singaporean, tries to visit every year. "I would rather visit my parents at this happy time than at any other time." May Lee says that the air is full of excitement, not just because it is New Year's but because nearly all the schools and many companies and communities come together to make floats for the parade. "The parade and the season help me keep in touch with my roots," she says.

【Notes】Chingay Parade「チンゲイ・パレード」、Chinese New Year「旧正月」、Chinese Singaporean「中国系シンガポール人」、happy「めでたい」、at any other time「他の時期」、air「雰囲気」、not A but B「AではなくB」、keep in touch with〜「〜と接触を保つ」

 (3)　Aging Japan is a continuing problem. Road accidents involving aged people seem to be on the rise. Some elderly people crossing streets are too weak to walk quickly. Older drivers don't have the quick reflexes of the young. They can't stop quickly in an emergency. Yes, the elderly can easily be caught up in an accident. Some politicians think that it is better for all people over 70 to give up their driver's license and use public transport. On the other hand, there are also many healthy, quick-minded 70 and 80-year-olds.

【Notes】aging「高齢化の」、continuing「現在進行中の」、aged people「高齢者」、on the rise「増加傾向で」、reflexes「反射能力」、the young「若者」、in an emergency「まさかのときに」、catch up in〜「〜に巻き込まれる」、public transport「公共交通機関」、quick-minded「頭の回転がよい」

Unit 15 分　詞（1）

次の各文を日本語に訳しなさい。

(1) It's Festival time again! Everyone, no matter where they are from, loves to party. In Brazil, people wearing bright colored costumes parade down the main street, dancing to the beat of the music. In Italy, people put on masks, and some also dress in elaborate costumes. In Australia, huge floats covered with flowers or fruit slowly move down the street. They display the products of the town. Scotland loves their marching bands. In Japan, people come to see young boys on galloping horses shoot arrows at a target. Others watch tall floats pass by.

【Notes】 **no matter A**「たとえAであろうと」、**party**「パーティーへ出かける」、**parade**「行進する」、**dance to the music**「音楽に合わせて踊る」、**elaborate**「豪華な」、**product**「産物」、**gallop**「疾走する」、**shoot arrows**「矢を射る」、**at~**「～をめがけて」、**pass by**「通り過ぎる」

(2) I walked into the travel agency and sat in front of a big poster of Tahiti. The shop was quite busy and I was kept waiting for at least ten minutes. When the agent finally came, we talked about the prices of trips to Taiwan. Suddenly, the poster began to sway to and fro. I felt the floor shaking. I heard a child scream behind me. "Earthquake!" I gasped. "It's a big one," I said clutching my bag and getting ready to run. The agent sat quietly, not looking nervous at all. The shaking soon stopped, and, as if nothing had happened, we continued to discuss the topic of trips to Taiwan.

【Notes】 **travel agency**「旅行代理店」、**quite**「かなり」、**keep ~ing**「～し続ける」、**agent**「店の人」、**finally**「ようやく」、**sway to and fro**「前後に揺れ動く」、**gasp**「息をのむ」、**get ready~**「～の用意をする」、**run**「逃げる」、**continue to do**「引き続き～する」

(3) Johnny ran all the way home. At school he had heard that a travelling circus was coming to town. Everyone became excited, and looked forward to the day. When the day arrived, Johnny and Grandpa went to watch the men and elephants pulling up the big tent. After lunch, they came again and caught a glimpse of a man practicing tricks with a bear. At six, the show began. They saw acrobats swinging high above their heads. They saw young girls do tricks on the backs of horses. They also saw a very funny clown run around the ring being chased by a clever monkey.

【Notes】 **all the way**「ずっと」、**traveling circus**「移動サーカス」、**pull up~**「～を引っ張り上げ（立ち上げ）る」、**catch a glimpse of~**「～を一目見る」、**trick**「曲芸」、**acrobat**「曲芸師」、**swing**「ブランコに乗る」、**run around**「走り回る」、**ring**「舞台」

Unit 16　分　詞（2）

次の各文を日本語に訳しなさい。

 (1)　It being sunny, I decided to go for a little excursion. I had no destination. I thought I would decide along the way. I got on the Yamanote Line and rode it for a while. Not seeing anything that interested me, I got out and took another train going north. As the train crossed the Arakawa, I thought I might like to explore that area more. I got out at Warabi and asked a passerby if there were any special sights to see there. He directed me to Sangaku Temple. Nearby I found an old shop called Manju-ya, selling delicious rice crackers.

【Notes】**go for~**「～に出かける」、**excursion**「小旅行」、**along the way**「途中で」、**explore~**「～を探検する」、**passerby**「通行人」、**if~**「～かどうか」、**sights**「名所」、**direct A to B**「AにBへ行く道を教える」、**rice cracker**「せんべい」

 (2)　Charlotte had not seen Donald for over five years, so why was she thinking of him now? Opening the top drawer of her desk, she took out his letter. It was the last one he had sent. There was no return address, but the postmark read 'Nairobi.' Why he had gone to Africa, she did not know. Suddenly, there was a knock at the door. Hearing a male voice call out her name, the letter fell from her trembling fingers. She ran to the door. There stood a tall man with a moustache. Who was he? Then she looked into the man's kind blue eyes and she knew it was Donald.

【Notes】**the top drawer of her desk**「彼女の机の一番上の引き出し」、**take out~**「～を取り出す」、**the last one** = the last letter、**return address**「差出人住所」、**postmark**「消印」、**read~**「～とある」、**call out~**「～を大声で叫ぶ」、**moustache**「口ひげ」、**look into~**「～をじっと見入る」

 (3)　Generally speaking, "Cool Japan" is a term used to mean interesting products made in Japan. The term was first used in 2002 in an article in the magazine Foreign Policy. Judging from the content of that and similar articles, we can see how popular the T.V. drama "Oshin" was at that time, and how Pokemon evolved. Later, the Japanese government used the term to try to 'sell' Japan to tourists. Some critics think that the Cool Japan Campaign was not successful. They say that even with a special Cool Japan budget, money was not given to young artists who needed it.

【Notes】**term**「用語」、**article**「記事」、**Foreign Policy**（国際情勢等を扱う雑誌名）、**"Oshin"**『おしん』（1983~4年放送の番組）、**evolve**「徐々に展開する」、**critic**「評論家」、**budget**「予算」

Unit 17　動名詞（1）

次の各文を日本語に訳しなさい。

(1)　It goes without saying that good health is the key to a long and happy life. The concept of good health is so important to us that some telephone companies provide Health Care software applications with a new telephone. One company sells a health care package that includes the four sections of Activity, Nutrition, Mindfulness, and Sleep. Walking is good for our health, so the Activity section includes a pedometer. Each day, it counts how many steps we take, how far we walk, and how many flights of stairs we climb.

【Notes】 **good health**「健康」、**key to~**「～のかぎ、秘訣」、**concept**「（商品の）テーマ」、**provide A with B**「AにBを提供する」、**health care package**「健康管理ソフト」、**Activity**「運動」、**Mindfulness**「心」、**pedometer**「歩数計（万歩計）」、**take steps**「（何）歩進む」、**a flight of stairs**「一続きの階段」

(2)　Anne and Brian lived in a little town on the east coast of Australia. Anne wanted to travel around the country. She had friends in central Australia and family in the west. Brian had friends in the north and family in the south. They decided to sell the house and buy a caravan. They also bought a big car to pull the caravan. First they went south. They continued living in the caravan and travelling around Australia for nearly ten years. They enjoyed visiting their friends and relatives, and also saw many famous sightseeing spots. After their long "holiday" they were ready to stay in one place again.

【Notes】 **travel around~**「～を周遊旅行する」、**caravan**「トレーラーハウス」、**pull~**「～を牽引する」、**be ready to do**「～する準備ができた」

(3)　"Where do you intend going this winter?" said Bob to his friend. Jack said that he wanted to go the U.K. "I promised to take my wife to Hawaii," Bob replied. "Would you like to join us?" he added.

　　Jack told Bob that his hobby was taking photographs of festivals. He explained that he wanted to go to Scotland to photograph Hogmanay, the New Year's festival in Edinburgh. "I remember going to Hawaii about five years ago. I don't like swimming or surfing, so I didn't enjoy the stay. I'm sorry, but Hawaii is not for me!" said Jack.

【Notes】 **intend~**「～するつもり」、**join~**「～と一緒に行く・なる」、**photograph~**「～の写真を撮る」、**Hogmanay**「ホグマネイ（スコットランドの大晦日から新年の祭り）」、**Edinburgh**「エディンバラ（スコットランドの首都）」、**I'm sorry, but~**「残念ながら～です」、**for~**「～に向いた」

Unit 18　動名詞（2）

次の各文を日本語に訳しなさい。

 (1)　I didn't feel like working last Monday, so I rang the office to say I wasn't feeling well. Then I took my surfboard and went to the beach with my friend, Doug. Doug and I spent about two hours at the beach and then, on the way home, we decided to rent a DVD. Just as I stepped into the video shop, I couldn't help feeling that someone was watching me. Next day at work, my boss called me into his office. "Jack, you should be more careful when walking about town when you are supposed to be sick." Of course, I denied it all, but I regret having lied to my boss.

【Notes】**on the way home**「家への帰り道に」、**step into~**「～に入る」、**about** = around「～のあたりを」、**be supposed to do**「～していることになっている」、**lie to~**「～にうそを言う」

 (2)　On retiring, Mr. Green was asked about his time with the company. "I've been the janitor here for over thirty years. One of the biggest changes has been the work environment. Now, the whole place is so clean. When I first came, there were cigarette butts everywhere, and the smoke was terrible for a man like me with asthma. Then they built smoking rooms. Now the whole building is a non-smoking area. Because of that, I'd like to say that my last year here has been the best," he laughed. "Now, if you could just stop hiding candy papers in the potted plants next to the elevators…."

【Notes】**one's time**「若い頃」、**janitor**「管理人」、**butt**「吸い殻」、**terrible**「つらい」、**stop hiding**「隠す（様に捨てる）のをやめる」、**candy paper**「アメの包み紙」、**potted plants**「鉢植えの木」

 (3)　Mohammed Ali put on his boxing gloves and confidently went into the boxing ring. It was September 5th, 1960. Ali, then known as Cassius Clay, beat his opponent from Poland and won a gold medal for the US at the Rome Olympics. The following month, he won his first fight as a professional. He went on to become a legend, winning 56 matches out of a total of 61 fights. He left boxing in 1984, and was diagnosed with Parkinson's syndrome that same year. Ali's last great feat was to light the Olympic Flame at the Opening Ceremony of the Centennial Olympics held in Atlanta in 1996.

【Notes】**Cassius Clay**「（イスラム教改宗前の名前）カシアス・クレイ」、**fight**「ボクシングの試合」、**go on to do**「続けて～する」、**leave~**「～をやめる」、**Parkinson's syndrome**「パーキンソン病」、**light~**「～に点火する」、**Flame**「聖火」、**centennial**「100周年記念の」、**hold~**「～を開催する」

Unit 19　形容詞・副詞

次の各文を日本語に訳しなさい。

(1)　Elizabeth Bisland could hardly believe her ears when the captain shouted "Japan!" All she could see was the top of a snow-capped mountain. Mt. Fuji rose above the waves. Then, slowly, the ship came closer and closer to the land. She saw other mountains and villages along the shore. Bisland landed in Yokohama, but could spend only 36 hours there on that first trip in 1889. She was racing around the world. However, Bisland was so impressed with the country that she visited Japan exactly four times during her life, and stayed a little longer each trip.

【Notes】**Elizabeth Bisland**「エリザベス・ビスランド」（1861~1929米国人ジャーナリスト）、**all**（代）「全てのもの」、**snow-capped**「雪を頂いた」、**rise above~**「～の上にそびえる」、**land**「上陸する」、**spend~**「～を過ごす」、**race around the world**「世界一周のタイムを争う」

(2)　Sapporo is a city famous for its Snow Festival. Replicas of important buildings, and huge statues of animals, people or cartoon characters line up along the main street. Visitors come from all over the world to see the spectacular display of snow art. The hotels are always full at this time of the year, so you'd better book early. If you can't afford a hotel, don't worry. The youth hostel is very near. After walking around the statues in the cold, frosty air, try some Sapporo Ramen noodles. They will warm you up from the inside.

【Notes】**replica**「複製」、**cartoon**「アニメ」、**line up**「並ぶ」、**spectacular**「壮大な」、**display**「展示」、**book**「予約する」、**can afford~**「～する金銭的余裕がある」、**youth hostel**「ユースホステル（安価な宿泊施設）」、**frosty**「凍るような寒さの」、**inside**「腹」

(3)　"You look tired, Rolf," said Gary. "Why are you standing out here in the hot sun?" Rolf replied that he was waiting for a certain friend to come. They hadn't seen each other in a long time, and had met unexpectedly at the festival a few days before. They had made a promise to meet at the park that day. "Clearly, she isn't here," said Gary sternly. "I think you've been stood up!" he added. That made Rolf sad. Just as they were about to leave the park Rolf's friend came running up to them. Rolf smiled but Gary couldn't hide his surprise. Rolf's friend was Gary's younger sister.

【Notes】**out**「外に出て」、**in a long time**「しばらくの間」、**sternly**「（顔つきが）厳しく」、**stand up**「（人との）約束をすっぽかす」、**be about to do**「～しようとしている」

Unit 20 比　較（1）

次の各文を日本語に訳しなさい。

 (1)　Hawaii is the 50th state. It is furthest from the capital Washington D.C. and is one of the most diverse. There you can experience summer all year round. On the biggest island, Hawai'i, you can find Mauna Kea, a mountain of over 4,000m. It is the highest mountain in the state. It even gets snow during winter. Hawai'i also has volcanoes. Kilauea is one of the most active volcanoes on earth. It is sometimes called "the world's only drive-in volcano" because you can drive close by, and watch the lava flowing into the sea.

【Notes】**state**「州」、**the capital Washington D.C.**「首都ワシントン、コロンビア特別区」、**diverse**「多様な」、**all year round**「1年中」、**find~**「～がある（ことを知る）」、**Kilauea**「キラウエア火山（2018年に再噴火）」、**on earth**「世界中で」、**drive-in**「乗り入れ式の」、**close by**「すぐ近くに」、**flow**「流れる」

 (2)　Which do you prefer, coffee or tea? Personally, I used to prefer tea to coffee. Many people believe that the English will only drink tea and Americans will only drink coffee. This belief probably came about because of the famous Boston Tea Party. The new settlers to Massachusetts were mostly from England and enjoyed drinking tea. But when England put a heavy tax on the tea, the people protested. The protesters throw boxes of tea, from the ship bringing them, into the bay. From then on, Americans began to drink more coffee.

【Notes】**the English**「イギリス人」、**belief**「考え」、**come about**「生じる」、**the Boston Tea Party**「ボストン茶会事件（1773年）」、**settler**「移住者」、**enjoy~**「～を（楽しく）味わう」、**put a tax on~**「～に税を課す」、**protest**「抗議する」、**from then on**「その時から」

 (3)　Have you ever wished that you could take another day off school or work? With 25 days, Sri Lanka has more public holidays per year than any other country. Japan has as many days as Thailand. South Korea and Taiwan have three days fewer than Japan. Australia and the U.S. have only 10 days, but in these two countries, each state also has a holiday for their State Fair. Mexico is the lowest with only seven public holidays. However, Mexico also has 14 civic holidays and 16 festival days that are not paid holidays. That shows that Mexicans love holidays as much as anyone else.

【Notes】**take a day off~**「一日～を休む」、**with~**「～を持っている、～ある」、**public holiday**「公休日、祝日」、**South Korea**「韓国」、**State Fair**「農産物・家畜品評会」、**civic**「市民の」、**as ~ as anyone else**「他の誰にも劣らず～」

Unit 21　比　較（2）

次の各文を日本語に訳しなさい。

(1)　Disney used to be equated with *Cinderella* and *Snow White*, romantic stories of pretty girls and handsome princes. It seems that Disney is changing with the times. *Mulan* features a Chinese girl as strong-willed as any soldier. *Frozen* ends with sisterly love. *Zootopia* shows that even small (lady) bunnies can be stronger than big (male) buffaloes. *Moana* tells how a chief's daughter is chosen to return a relic to a goddess, and even a demi-god like Maui isn't as smart as Moana. The women in modern Disney animation are stronger and more powerful than ever before.

【Notes】**equate A with B**「AをBと同じと考える」、**with the times**「時がたつにつれて」、**feature~**「~を主演俳優とする」、**strong-willed**「意思の強い」、*Frozen*「アナと雪の女王」、**sisterly love**「姉妹愛」、**chief**「村長」、**choose to do**「~することに決める」、**relic**「心」、**demi-god**「半神半人」

(2)　"So you like classical music!" said Bob looking at the CD Susan was holding.
　"Do you know Seiji Ozawa? He was a most skillful conductor!" replied Susan.
　"Oh, yes. And do you know Leonard Bernstein? He is the conductor I admire most. I tried to buy at least one of his CDs every year when I was young. He was so much more than just a conductor though. He was a wonderful composer, too."
　"Of course, nothing can compare to Bernstein's *West Side Story*," said Susan. "But personally, I prefer Mozart. No composer interests me as much as Mozart," she added.

【Notes】**most skillful**「実にうまい」、**conductor**「指揮者」、**admire most**「いちばん尊敬する」、**more than~**「~以上の人」、**though**「けれど」、*West Side Story*『（ミュージカル映画）ウエストサイド物語』、**no... as much as~**「~ほど…する（人）はいない」

(3)　Garfield is no more intelligent than the average child. He is perhaps a little lazier, and he probably likes lasagna more than the average child, but Garfield is nothing special. Garfield is the chubby cat that appears in a cartoon strip by the same name. However, although Garfield is less active than most household cats, he has one trait that has led to him being called Professor Garfield. Now, more and more children are learning to enjoy reading through Professor Garfield's home page, and by borrowing books from mobile libraries decorated with pictures of Garfield.

【Notes】**lazy**「ものぐさな」、**lasagna**「（料理）ラザーニャ」、**cartoon strip**「漫画」、**household**「家庭にいる」、**trait**「特質」、**lead to~**「~となる」、**more and more**「ますます多くの」、**mobile library**「移動図書館」、**decorate A with B**「AをBで飾る」

Unit 22　前置詞

次の各文を日本語に訳しなさい。

(1)　Ron and Terry asked their mother if they could go and play in the sand pit. "Okay, but be back by five," their mother replied. The brothers took some playthings and went out to play. But the place where the brothers played was not like most sand pits. It was under a highway bridge, just 10 meters from a railway. The "sand" was fine gravel. It was full of stones. The boys decorated their stone towers and sand castles with crow feathers and autumn leaves. Ron liked his pocket-sized playground, but Terry wished he could play in the fields, on his grandfather's farm.

【Notes】**sand pit**「砂場」、**plaything**「遊び道具」、**most**「たいていの」、**fine gravel**「細かな砂利」、**autumn leaves**「枯葉」、**pocket-sized**「狭い」、**field**「牧草地」、**farm**「農場」

(2)　In 2018, India became joyous over winning its first medal in skiing. When you think of India, few people would think of snow and winter sport. But as Aanchal Thakur, the winner of the bronze medal for slalom at an international skiing event in Turkey says, "We have the Himalayas, so why not?" In an interview, Thakur's father praised his daughter's effort. Even the Prime Minister congratulated her in a twitter message. Her win was significant. Up until then India had only one or two male representatives.

【Notes】**joyous**「喜びに満ちた」、**over~**「~に関して」、**think of~**「~を考える」、**Aanchal Thakur**「アーンチャル・タクル」、**winner of the bronze medal**「銅メダリスト」、**Why not?**「どうしてだめなのか、良いでしょう」

(3)　In spite of its long snowy winters, the people of Oslo like to walk in the park. Their favorite park would have to be Frogner Park, near the center of the city. The park has more than 200 granite and bronze statues made by Gustav Vigeland. The statues are of men, women and children in various poses. The statues range from the very young to the very old. Children laugh and cry. The young men show strong muscles. Women play with babies. The aged are weak and grieve death. In the center of the display is a great monolith, some 17 meters high.

【Notes】**snowy**「雪の多い」、**Frogner Park**「フログネル公園」、**granite**「みかげ石（の）」、**bronze statue**「銅像」、**Gustav Vigeland**「グスタフ・ヴィゲラント」、**pose**「ポーズ」、**range from A to B**「AからBに及ぶ」、**the young**「若者」、**grieve death**「死を悲しむ」、**monolith**「一本石の柱」

Unit 23　関係詞（1）

次の各文を日本語に訳しなさい。

(1)　A hand patted me on the back and a voice said, "Claude! You are just the person I wanted to see." I turned towards the voice. I knew it was Tom, an old friend from High School. Tom was loud. He spoke in a loud voice. He laughed loudly. Even his footsteps were louder than anyone else's. Tom was also cheery and always offered to help others. But there was a catch to his kind offers. "I know a man whose wife runs a small kindergarten," he said. "They are looking for someone to help them fix the roof. I told them that you would love to give them a hand." I could not refuse Tom.

【Notes】**pat A on the back**「Aの背中を軽くたたく」、**loud**「騒々しい」、**cheery**「陽気な」、**offer to do**「〜しようと申し出る」、**others**「他の人」、**catch**「わな」、**give A a hand**「Aに手を貸す」

(2)　"Now this is the street which goes by the name of the Miracle Mile," said the guide as we turned into the avenue called Kokusai Dori in Japanese. "Why is it called that?" she asked us. Without waiting for an answer, she began to explain how the road was just a path through a swamp. But after the war, the men and women who had lost their livelihood during the war began to revive the town. In no time at all, Kokusai Dori became Okinawa's most popular shopping street. In a street that is nearly one mile long, you can find nearly every kind of shop: from shoe shops to fish markets!

【Notes】**go by the name of~**「〜の名前で知られている」、**turn**「（〜へ）向かう」、**avenue**「大通り」、**how**「なんと」、**path**「小道」、**livelihood**「生計」、**revive~**「〜を復興させる」、**in no time at all**「すぐに」

(3)　It was dusk when Misa and her daughter Saki left the violin teacher's house. They drove along the same road that they travelled every Thursday, but today, Saki spotted something new. "Tokyo Tower!" she shouted suddenly. In fact, as Saki's family lived in a rural town, the telephone tower that she saw was far shorter than the real Tokyo Tower. However, for a little girl who had just turned five, the brightly lit tower was the nearest thing to pictures she had seen on television. It was then that Misa promised Saki that they would go to Tokyo during the next spring holidays.

【Notes】**dusk**「夕暮れ」、**along~**「〜に沿って」、**travel**「通う」、**something new**「何か新しいもの」、**brightly lit**「明るく輝いている」、**near**「よく似た」、**picture**「画像」、**It is...that~**（強調構文）

Unit 24　関係詞（2）

次の各文を日本語に訳しなさい。

(1)　Last year, I went with my father to Holland. We visited the house where he was born. Dad told me a story about what happened in that house one day. It was wartime in Europe. The sirens had gone off and so Grandma took Dad, who was only about three at the time, downstairs. The cellar, in those days, was the safest place. Then a bomb came plunging through the roof and into the kitchen stove. It was a phosphorous bomb, or what we call a fire bomb. Luckily it stayed in the stove, and luckily my Grandpa had sandbags ready to put out the fire.

【Notes】**wartime**「戦時」、**go off**「鳴る」、**downstairs**「階下に」、**cellar**「地下室」、**plunge through A and into B**「Aを通過してBに飛び込む」、**stove**「コンロ」、**phosphorous bomb**「白リン弾」、**fire bomb**「焼夷弾」、**have A ready**「Aを用意しておく」、**put out~**「～を消す」

(2)　"Moon Beach is the only place I can relax," said Tom, head of a major trading company. "When it was new, this hotel was the talk of the town. It's spacious, and what's more, perfect for the family." As he strolled along the beach, a little girl came running up to him. "Show me what you have in your hands," he said gently. The little girl opened her hands to show her grandfather her treasure of coral and shells. Tom waved to a boy splashing about in the outdoor pool. "These kids are the reason why my staff don't contact me when I'm at Moon Beach."

【Notes】**head**「社長」、**talk**「話題」、**perfect for~**「～にうってつけ」、**stroll**「散歩する」、**run up**「駆け寄る」、**wave**「手を振り挨拶する」、**splash about**「水をはね散らす」、**contact~**「～に連絡する」

(3)　The year 2018 was the year that Japan celebrated 150 years of modernity. It had been 150 years since the Meiji Restoration. In Kyushu, they arranged events around the people who played important roles at the time, including Saigo Takamori. Elsewhere, museums put on displays that showed the art, fashion, and lifestyle of the era. Even the Japan Camera Museum in Tokyo showed how cameras had developed over the years. In the Railway Museum, people were able to look at old photos and drawings, some that dated as far back as 1864.

【Notes】**modernity**「近代化」、**Meiji Restoration**「明治維新」、**arrange~**「～を計画する」、**around** = about、**play a role**「役目を果たす」、**put on~**「～を行う」、**display**「展示」、**show~**「～を紹介する」、**over the years**「長年にわたり」、**date as far back as~**「古くは～までさかのぼる」

Unit 25　仮定法（1）

次の各文を日本語に訳しなさい。

(1)　Yuri's grandmother's voice rose as she started to tell us about the war. "If I had stayed in that cave, I would have been killed," she said. Yuri's grandmother was a student when the war broke out. First, they planted vegetables for the soldiers. Soon, she and her friends were told to help care for the soldiers in hospital. As more and more bombs fell, people began to hide in caves. "If my father had listened to my mother, we might have escaped to Kyushu, but we stayed here in Okinawa. As a result, I saw my parents die, and I lost many of my friends. War is terrible. We must try to keep peace," she said.

【Notes】rise「（声が）高まる」、**cave**「洞窟」、**break out**「始まる」、**help do**「〜するのを手伝う」、**care for~**「〜の看護をする」、**try to do**「〜しようとがんばる」

(2)　Miho had wanted to be a teacher since she was in Grade 6. Her Grade 6 teacher, Mr. Azuma, was very kind to her. He was very clever, too. Miho wanted to help children learn the way Mr. Azuma had helped her learn. When Miho was in university, her professor thought she should try something different. "If I were you," he said, "I would become a writer." Miho liked writing, so she got a job with a newspaper. She stayed there for almost ten years, but she couldn't forget her dream. She left the newspaper. Soon she will start her new life as a teacher.

【Notes】Grade 6「小学校6年生」、**help A B~**「AがBするのを助ける」、**way**「〜のように」、**writer**「（新聞）記者」、**get a job with~**「〜に入社する」、**newspaper**「新聞社」

(3)　"If you started the walk by this afternoon, you should be able to cross the mountains before it rains," advised Roy's aunt. But first the two men had a long train ride to complete before starting their hike from Miyama to Wakasa. The typhoon struck sooner than expected. After four hours on the train, the train suddenly stopped. The tracks were under water. One night on the train and one day in Kyoto later, the men started their mountain hike. The hiking trail was very bad. "If we hadn't found that forest road, and if someone hadn't stopped for us, we could have died there!" Roy said later.

【Notes】cross~「〜を越える」、**a long train ride**「長い列車の旅」、**complete~**「〜を終える、行う」、**hike**「徒歩旅行」、**strike**「襲う」、**sooner than expected**「予想していたより早く」、**tracks** = railway tracks、**under water**「浸水して」、**forest road**「森林道」

Fundamental English Grammar

Unit 26　仮定法（2）

次の各文を日本語に訳しなさい。

 (1)　　Ted was in trouble. Big trouble. Reporters knocked at the door. At the first knock, early in the morning, mother had answered the door. Immediately, cameras flashed. Mother was shocked. To Ted she said, "Had I been in your place, I would have told the truth. Even if you are with friends, you should never lie to the police!" Mother looked as if she had been crying all night. Ted wished he had made better friends when they had moved to this new town. He had not realized that the new comic books his new friends had were all stolen.

【Notes】**be in trouble**「トラブルに巻き込まれている」、**reporter**「記者」、**answer the door**「玄関に対応に出る」、**flash**「ピカッと光る」、**in one's place**「〜の立場」、**realize~**「〜に気がつく」

 (2)　　"If not for you, my sky would fall. Rain would gather, too." Bob Dylan's song came from the speakers of my car radio. "Without your love, I'd be nowhere at all." The song lasted but a few minutes, but the words echoed in my head all day long. Lily was like her name: elegant, pure, friendly, always smiling. She was like sunshine to me. But for her advice to go overseas, I would never have tried to learn English in earnest, and I would never have found the job I'm in now. But what should I do now? If only I had brought Lily with me to England! Then we might still be together.

【Notes】**"If…too."**「君がいないと、空は垂れさがり。雨も降るよ」、**"Without…all"**「君の愛がないと、ぼくの居場所はまったくない」、**but** = only、**echo**「繰り返される」、**like~**「〜のような」、**in earnest**「本気で」、**in~**「〜従事して」、**bring A to B**「AをBに連れてくる」

 (3)　　It was Dave's first visit to New Zealand. On his bucket list, he had: visit a hot spa, hug a kauri tree, see a live kiwi, and swim in the Pacific Ocean. Coming from Ireland, Dave was especially eager to do the last item. "Were it a little warmer, we could swim in the sea," said his host. "But let's go to Hot Water Beach instead," he added. So off they went to the Coromandel Peninsular. "I wish I had a spade to dig my own hot spa pool," said Dave watching others digging in the white sand. They hired a spade, dug a hole, and relaxed. Dave checked off two items in one afternoon.

【Notes】**bucket list**「やるべき事の一覧表」、**kauri**「（植）カウリマツ」、**kiwi**（鳥）、**be eager to do**「〜することを熱望して」、**item**「項目」、**go off**「出発する」、**the Coromandel Peninsular**「コーラマンデル半島」、**spade**「スコップ」、**check off~**「〜に終了済みの印を入れる」

読解力につなげるコア英文法

検印省略	© 2019年1月31日　初版発行
	2024年1月31日　第3刷発行

著　者　　　　　　　　　　福井　慶一郎
　　　　　　　　　　　山中　マーガレット
　　　　　　　　　　　　　　北山　長貴

発行者　　　　　　　　　　　原　雅久

発行所　　　　　株式会社　朝 日 出 版 社
　　　　101-0065　東京都千代田区西神田 3-3-5
　　　　　　電話　東京 (03) 3239-0271/72
　　　　　　FAX　東京 (03) 3239-0479
　　　　　e-mail　text-e@asahipress.com
　　　　　　振替口座　00140-2-46008
　　　組版／クロス・コンサルティング　製版／錦明印刷

乱丁・落丁はお取り替えいたします。
ISBN978-4-255-15638-5　C1082

ちょっと手ごわい、でも効果絶大！
最強のリスニング強化マガジン

CNN ENGLISH EXPRESS

音声ダウンロード付き　毎月6日発売　定価1,263円（本体1,148円＋税10%）

英語が楽しく続けられる！

重大事件から日常のおもしろネタ、スターや著名人のインタビューなど、CNNの多彩なニュースを生の音声とともにお届けします。3段階ステップアップ方式で初めて学習する方も安心。どなたでも楽しく続けられて実践的な英語力が身につきます。

資格試験の強い味方！

ニュース英語に慣れれば、TOEIC®テストや英検のリスニング問題も楽に聞き取れるようになります。

定期購読をお申し込みの方には本誌1号分無料ほか、特典多数。詳しくは下記ホームページへ。

CNN ENGLISH EXPRESS ホームページ

英語学習に役立つコンテンツが満載！

[本誌のホームページ] https://ee.asahipress.com/
[編集部のTwitter] https://twitter.com/asahipress_ee

朝日出版社　〒101-0065 東京都千代田区西神田 3-3-5　TEL 03-3263-3321

生きた英語でリスニング!

CNN ニュース・リスニング 2022［春夏］
電子書籍版付き（ダウンロード方式で提供）

1本30秒だから、聞きやすい！

［30秒×3回聞き］方式で
世界標準の英語がだれでも聞き取れる！

- 羽生結弦、「氷上の王子」の座はゆずらない
- オックスフォード英語辞典にKカルチャー旋風
- 「母語」と「外国語」を犬も聞き分けている！…など

MP3音声・電子書籍版付き
（ダウンロード方式）
A5判 定価1100円（税込）

初級者からのニュース・リスニング
CNN Student News 2022［夏秋］

音声アプリ+動画で、どんどん聞き取れる！
- レベル別に2種類の速度の音声を収録
- ニュース動画を字幕あり/なしで視聴できる

MP3・電子書籍版・
動画付き［オンライン提供］
A5判 定価1,320円（税込）

朝日出版社 〒101-0065 東京都千代田区西神田 3-3-5　TEL 03-3263-3321

GLobal ENglish Testing System

大学生向け団体受験用テスト

CNN GLENTS Basic

グローバル英語力を測定
新時代のオンラインテスト

詳しくはWEBで！

https://www.asahipress.com/special/glents/organization/

銀行のセミナー・研修でお使いいただいています

Point 01
生の英語ニュースが素材

Point 02
場所を選ばず受験できるオンライン方式

Point 03
自動採点で結果をすぐに表示、
国際指標CEFRにも対応

※画像はイメージです。

テストを受けてくださった学生のみなさまの反応

◇生の英語でのテストは非常に優位性があると思いました。
◇動画問題があるのが面白い！
◇将来海外に行くときに直接役立つと感じました。
◇音声を聞くことができる回数が1回のみだったので、
　真の「聞いて理解する力」を試されていると思いました。
◇多様な生の英語に慣れておく必要性を感じる良い経験となりました。

これからの大学生に求められる英語とは

企業が求める英語力はどんどん変化しています。これからの社会人は、違う文化を持つ人々と英語でしっかりコミュニケーションを取る必要があり、異文化に対する知識・理解を増やす必要があります。ですから、それらを身につけるために生の英語＝CNN GLENTS Basicで英語力を測り、CNNをはじめ様々なメディアで勉強することは非常に効果の高い学習法だと感じていますし、お勧めします。

鈴木武生氏

東京大学大学院総合文化研究科修了（言語情報科学専攻）。専門は英語、中国語、日本語の意味論。1991年にアジアユーロ言語研究所を設立。企業向けスキル研修、翻訳サービスなどを手掛ける。

受験料：大学生1人あたり2,200円（税込）　受験料は、受けていただく学生の人数によってご相談させていただきます。

株式会社 朝日出版社「CNN GLENTS」事務局　☎0120-181-202　✉glents_support@asahipress.com

® & © Cable News Network A WarnerMedia Company. All Rights Reserved.